SECOND EDITION

HOW TO PROTECT YOUR MONEY OFFSHORE

Arnold S. Goldstein, J.D., LL.M., Ph.D.

GARRETT PUBLISHING, INC.

HOW TO PROTECT YOUR MONEY OFFSHORE
(SECOND EDITION)
By Arnold S. Goldstein, J.D., LL.M., Ph.D.
Copyright 2000 by Garrett Publishing, Inc.

Published by Garrett Publishing, Inc.
384 S. Military Trail
Deerfield Beach, FL 33442
954-480-8543 (Phone)
954-698-0057 (Fax)

This publication is designed to provide accurate and authoritative information in regard to the subject matter covered. It is sold with the understanding that neither the publisher nor the author is engaged in rendering the legal, accounting, or other professional service. If legal advice or other expert assistance is required, the services of a competent professional should be sought. *From A Declaration of Principals jointly adopted by the Committee of the American Bar Association and a Committee of Publishers.*

Library of Congress Cataloging-in-publication Data

Goldstein, Arnold S.
    How to Protect Your Money Offshore
    p.   cm.
    Includes bibliographical references.
    ISBN   1-880539-59-4
    1. Asset protection. 2. Banks and banking, International. 3. Banks and banking, foreign. 4. Banks and banking — United States. 5. Privacy. 6. Tax Havens.
I. Title

Printed in the United States of America
10 9 8 7 6 5 4 3 2

"It's not difficult to make money today...

the trick is to keep it!"

FROM THE PUBLISHER

One of America's leading wealth protection specialists reveals his secrets and strategies for ironclad offshore financial protection.

Dr. Arnold S. Goldstein has helped thousands of individuals, families, and organizations gain complete financial protection. Through this special interview, he discusses his newest and most advanced strategies.

Perhaps you have seen or heard Dr. Goldstein discuss his powerful offshore financial strategies on radio and TV talk shows (including CNN, CNBC, and NBC's "Today Show"), or as a seminar and meeting speaker.

Or you possibly read about his offshore wealth-preservation concepts in numerous business and finance magazines . . . Inc . . . Fortune . . . Money . . . CFO . . . Entrepreneur . . . Success . . . Venture . . . Business Week . . . Bottom Line . . . to name a few.

You possibly may have found your path to financial security from his best-selling *Offshore Havens*,

Asset Protection Secrets, or his many other books on wealth protection.

A veteran wealth preservation attorney, Dr. Goldstein is the founder of the Florida and Massachusetts firm of Arnold S. Goldstein & Associates, a member of the Massachusetts and federal bars, and a member of the bar of the U.S. First Circuit Court and U.S. Supreme Court.

He holds five academic degrees (including graduate law degrees, an MBA and a Ph.D. in economic and business policy from Northeastern University where he is professor emeritus). He also served on the faculty at several other universities and as a post-doctoral research scholar on offshore trusts at the London School of Economics.

He is a member of the Offshore Institute, American and Massachusetts Bar Association, International Association of Financial Planning, International Tax Planning Association, and numerous other professional organizations. One of America's leading experts on offshore asset protection and other international and domestic strategies to conserve wealth, Dr. Goldstein invites his readers to reach him at (954) 420-4990 or visit his web page at: www.asgoldstein.com.

READERS' NOTE

In this *WealthSaver Organization* interview, we are pleased to have Dr. Arnold S. Goldstein answer the most commonly asked questions about a most important and timely subject: How to achieve offshore financial protection and security.

This publication is intended only to answer commonly asked questions about offshore wealth protection, and to provide a basic overview and general information on this topic. It is not designed to provide legal or other professional advice. In all instances, you should obtain legal or tax advice from a qualified practitioner before acting on any information in this book. Neither the publisher nor author can accept liability arising from the use of information in this book. While the information is believed to be accurate at the time of publication, laws do change and interpretations may vary.

Nothing herein should be interpreted as encouraging the violation of any present or future tax laws or other laws of any country. Certain strategies and concepts in this book may not comply with the laws of your country.

A PERSONAL WORD
FROM
ARNOLD S. GOLDSTEIN, Ph.D.

Thank you for taking a few moments to read this
book.

I hope that you will agree that it was time well spent
and an opportunity to obtain information about a
most important subject—protecting your hard-
earned wealth and safeguarding your family's financial
future.

I interviewed for this book because there is too little
accurate information and too much misinformation
about offshore finance, particularly in my own
professional field of offshore wealth preservation.
Information that is available and accurate is
oftentimes too technical to be useful to the layperson
seeking easily-understood answers to basic questions.
For that reason, my publisher, the WealthSaver
Organization and I thought a primer directly
answering the more common inquiries could
immeasurably help more people decide whether
offshore wealth protection can benefit them, illustrate
how it functions, and outline how they may correctly
go about it.

Certainly, no book can adequately answer every question or prescribe your one best course to help you accomplish this goal. You will need professional assistance. I would be pleased to consult with you on your specific needs and help you design and implement your customized wealth protection program following a professional, confidential consultation. If you would simply like to find out more about our services and how we can help you, please call for a "no-cost, no-obligation" confidential telephone or office appointment with myself or one of our staff attorneys.

It can be your most important first step to achieving true financial security for you and your family.

Arnold S. Goldstein, Ph.D.

Arnold S. Goldstein & Associates, P.A.
384 S. Military Trail
Deerfield Beach, Florida 33442
(954) 420-4990
e-mail: asgoldstein@mindspring.com
web: www.asgoldstein.com

TABLE OF CONTENTS

PREFACE:

Why You Must Read This Book Today! 13

SECTION ONE:

Offshore Financial Protection Planning 21

SECTION TWO:

Offshore Financial Privacy 61

SECTION THREE:

Offshore Trusts...77

SECTION FOUR:

More Offshore Wealth Protection Strategies 117

SECTION FIVE:

Getting Started 143

INDEX 155

WHY YOU MUST READ THIS BOOK TODAY!

"Life," John F. Kennedy once said, "isn't always fair. Even the venal can get rich."

"And, of course, the virtuous can as easily get poor."

That reality hit my old Army pal Charlie smack between the eyes when the IRS demanded he pay $475,000. Charlie, a part-owner of a business that folded several years earlier, was personally liable for its unpaid withholding taxes. His partner? Dead and buried. Charlie knew absolutely nothing about the firm's finances but nevertheless was left holding the bag.

Within three months Charlie had lost everything... his savings... expensive home... two cars... a vacation condo... even his pension. At 52, Charlie had only his family and faithful retriever, Sam.

The IRS blitz financially and emotionally devastated Charlie and his wife Martha. Too depressed to work, he and Martha scrimp by on Martha's pittance salary as a supermarket cashier. Charlie's two kids quit college, and Charlie and Martha are one step away from welfare.

It's mighty tough to think you're financially secure only to be suddenly wiped out. Ask Charlie!

Charlie's only one casualty. My next door neighbor recently lost his business and creditors seized his $300,000 savings. His nest egg is gone forever! My stockbroker? His wife abandoned him and walked away with $140,000 in cash and securities.

Two of my golfing pals, directors of a large corporations, are fighting $20 million lawsuits that several stockholders filed against them. With no insurance and a lifetime accumulation of assets, Henry and Ben have plenty to lose.

Big lawsuits. Business failure. Tax troubles. Divorce.

You too can feel safe and secure today and be suddenly wiped out tomorrow. You are now vulnerable and will remain vulnerable unless you protect yourself. Financial disaster can destroy your future unless you act now to shelter what you own. There's no way to avoid it. Today there are just too many ways to get into financial trouble because too many people want their grubby hands in your pocket. That is how it is in today's America, and it will get worse in the years ahead.

There are plenty of people like Charlie . . . oblivious to the reality that they too can be financially sideswiped when least expected.

These are people—probably people very much like yourself—who know how to make money in their own business or profession but have absolutely no idea how to protect their wealth. But protecting wealth is what I *do* know and what I will reveal to you in this book. I want you to see how offshore asset protection and wealth-preservation can give you more financial security in these unsafe times as it has for so many other farsighted Americans.

CIRCLE THE WAGONS

Like myself and so many others, you may not like the world as it has become. But you cannot change it. All you can do is protect yourself so that you can survive in the world as it is.

To survive you will need your very own financial self-defense plan, a plan that can protect:

- everything you own

- against any financial or legal threat

You cannot afford to settle for less. But the probability is that you now have no wealth protection plan. If your wealth is still exposed and vulnerable, you are not alone. *Nine out of ten American families with a net worth over $500,000 have absolutely no financial protection!*

That's why I want to show you a new and superior way to safeguard your assets against financial threat and to help you and your family enjoy the same lifetime financial security that so many of my clients now enjoy.

How to Protect Your Money Offshore reveals proven offshore strategies that can protect you as it has thousands of other individuals from every walk of life who wanted their wealth sheltered against financial crisis. The strategy in this book was their blueprint to an impenetrable financial fortress against lawsuits . . . creditors . . . bankruptcy . . . the IRS . . . divorce . . . probate . . . and so many other wealth-destroyers that we must all vigorously guard against.

You'll find this book vital whether or not you now have a financial protection plan. If your assets are presently unprotected, you'll discover how to build your financial fortress from scratch. If you think your assets are now well protected, you may find a far more powerful wealth-saving strategy. Either way, you have in your hands your key to the financially secure future that we all want but few achieve.

JOIN THE UNTOUCHABLES

Of course, there are many legal strategies that one can use to protect wealth. With 30 years in the trenches as an asset protection lawyer, I have used each and every one to protect my clients' assets, and I invented some of my own. My best-selling *Asset Protection Secrets* reveals over 300 proven ways to protect assets with the familiar domestic trusts, limited partnerships, corporations, co-tenancies, state exemptions and the many other wealth-preservation tactics.

The problem is that most of these conventional asset protection strategies are like hunting elephants with a BB gun. When a sue-happy lawyer comes after you or Uncle Sam eyeballs your bank account, you need *stronger* protection.

You must also do more than simply shelter your assets from those who want them. You must also privatize your wealth and keep a low profile. But you know how impossible that is in a cyber-tech age where your financial life is an open book.

Whether or not you have found it difficult to make money in America, you will find it nearly impossible to *keep* it in America. What was once the land of financial opportunity is now overrun by hordes of avaricious lawyers and litigants and armies of faceless bureaucrats who share one unmistakable objective: *your* wealth!

You need no shocking stories, statistics and revelations to prove the point. Simply open your eyes.

REGAINING YOUR FINANCIAL FREEDOM

My many years as an asset protection and wealth preservation lawyer taught me one critical lesson! **The safest way to hold wealth today is offshore.**

I have established offshore asset protection programs for hundreds of very grateful clients. None has lost one dime of their offshore assets to *any* financial threat. Moreover, these now financially secure people enjoy *greater* privacy and more profitable investments.

You will ask whether protecting your money offshore is *safe*. Rest assured, your money is far safer offshore than here in America.

You will ask whether it is *legal*. Rest assured, it is 100-percent legitimate.

You will ask whether it *works*. For that answer, ask a few of the tens of thousands of Americans who now have nearly four trillion dollars secured offshore. *They* make my case!

But all new ideas and concepts meet resistance and skepticism. For most people who need offshore protection, the obstacles will always be *ignorance* and *fear*.

You also may have been programmed to believe that offshore finance is only for crooks, frauds or the super-rich. Your own financial planner, lawyer and accountant will probably advise you to forget about it. They will tell you it's "too risky, too expensive, too bothersome." Odds are they don't know one thing more about offshore wealth protection than you do. But you will know considerably more about it once you read this book.

Offshore wealth protection is gradually gaining recognition, and it will continue to do so as financial professionals seek better ways to protect their clients' wealth. But learning takes time and you don't have time. You need protection *right now*!

I use a Q&A format because it's the easiest way to digest complex subjects. I am asked these same important questions time and again from clients and seminar attendees, and so I can accurately predict your questions. Please call me if I overlooked or failed to adequately answer an important question. I would be delighted to chat because I enjoy helping people gain the financial freedom they need and deserve!

FINANCIAL PROTECTION PLANNING

1

Dr. Goldstein, what do you mean by "wealth protection"?

Wealth protection shields your assets from danger. Mostly we mean protection against direct predatory threats such as lawsuits, governmental seizures, divorce, the IRS, and others who may seize your assets. The broader definition includes wealth erosion through economic hazards: inflation, deflation, poor investments, and taxes. Protection against economic hazards is the role of the investment advisor. My professional role is to protect my clients against direct predators.

What predatory threats concern most people?

The litigation explosion, of course, makes us all aware of the need for solid asset protection. My clients primarily want protection against lawsuits. It's not surprising, considering the five-fold increase in lawsuits since 1960.

Frivolous lawsuits have become all-too-common. Litigants frequently extort payment through our courts and juries. You never know how you'll end up on a case. You can't take a chance today. You can't always avoid lawsuits, but you can protect yourself against a bad outcome. However, a good asset protection program will do more than protect your wealth; it will also discourage lawsuits because you no longer have "deep pockets" that attract prospective litigants.

Lawsuits are hardly the only concern. We now see many more seizures by the SEC, FTC, and other governmental regulatory and law enforcement agencies. Our government has become nearly as big a threat to your pocketbook as avaricious lawyers. For instance, twenty million Americans owe the IRS. How safe are their assets?

Divorce? More dismal statistics. One-in-two marriages fail, and certainly divorce requires good financial self-defense planning, both before and after the marriage.

Bankruptcies tripled since 1990 to 1.5 million last year. How can you legally protect yourself today if you run into creditor troubles tomorrow? My clients want to protect themselves from these and the many other threats to their financial security emerging from so many different directions. Unfortunately, we have become a predatory society. The challenge is not amassing wealth, but keeping it!

Dr. Goldstein, you talk about protecting "wealth." Is this only for the rich?

"Wealth" is a misleading term. "Assets" is more accurate. But like most things, wealth is relative. An elderly chap recently came to me for asset protection. He shines shoes at a local airport and probably never earned over $25,000 a year. After 30 years at the shoeshine stand, Jim amassed a modest $60,000 net worth. Now you may not consider that "wealth," but for Jim it represented a lifetime of work and his financial security. Protecting Jim's nest egg was very important to him and it was money Jim could never recoup if he lost it.

I have many rich and famous clients, but most people who come to me for wealth protection are neither rich nor famous; they are everyday folks—doctors, plumbers, retailers, developers—mainstream Americans from virtually every occupation, age group, and background. They share one goal: to protect what they own.

So, "Who needs asset protection?" The answer, of course, is anyone with assets they wouldn't want to lose. It's not only for the wealthy.

Do only Americans worry about these financial dangers?

Of course not. People everywhere want financial security and safety for themselves, their families, and their businesses.

Obviously, Americans are considerably more concerned about lawsuits because litigation isn't as much a problem elsewhere, although it is rapidly rising in Canada and the United Kingdom. On the other hand, nationals from other countries were historically more endangered by governmental confiscations, seldom a concern to Americans only a few decades ago. But as foreigners experience more lawsuits, we are increasingly endangered by government. Divorce and bankruptcy are international problems. People everywhere want privacy, tax advantages, and international investment opportunities, which also fuels the offshore movement.

Can asset protection discourage litigation?

Absolutely. First, it helps to privatize your wealth. You no longer advertise your "deep pockets." This stops many potential lawsuits, as you are less a target for lawyers and litigants.

Second, a good asset protection plan should convince any litigant that it would be difficult, if not impossible, to collect even if his lawsuit succeeds. If you do get sued, you gain the leverage to settle on more favorable terms. The fastest, surest way to stop today's litigation explosion is for more Americans to protect their assets. When you can't easily get someone's money, you don't try.

America's wealthy are prime lawsuit targets because prospective litigants know that they will pay rather than fight. It's cheaper with today's exorbitant lawyer's fees, and who can risk a devastating loss? Litigation is always a "crapshoot."

Asset protection levels the playing field, stopping the plaintiff from collecting even if he sues and wins. That's incentive for a sensible plaintiff to settle early or for less, or not to sue at all.

Won't liability insurance adequately protect you?

No. Insurance only covers a narrow range of claims and for limited amounts. Insurance can't possibly cover the many potential liabilities, and claims frequently exceed policy limits.

Your insurance company may also go bankrupt and leave you uninsured. Moreover, your insurer can raise defenses to avoid a claim, such as if you violate a law or the claim falls within the many exclusions in your policy.

Insurance can protect against many foreseeable dangers, but for complete protection you must supplement insurance with other wealth protection strategies. You can't count on insurance alone to protect you.

Conversely, insurance makes you a more attractive target for lawsuits because a litigant knows he can recover from an insurance company, who becomes your "deep pocket." That's why so many physicians and other professionals now "go bare" without insurance. Aside from saving premiums, they attract fewer malpractice suits, because their patients see no easy way to collect. Insurance fuels litigation. Asset protection discourages and reduces it.

Dr. Goldstein, while anyone with assets apparently needs asset protection, how many people actually have their assets well protected?

Too few. People believe that financial disasters, like serious illness or death, happen only to others until they get whacked in the pocketbook. We don't seriously think about financial vulnerability until we become threatened. It's usually a good scare that chases people into my office. That's human nature, I suppose. We live in a world of optimists. They lose their money. Pessimists keep theirs.

Shouldn't a professional advisor caution their clients to protect themselves?

When people lose their assets, some blame may rest with their advisors. For instance, has your financial planner discussed asset protection with you? Few do. They make money selling investments, not protecting investments.

Lawyers are the big culprits. For example, a friend recently acquired an apartment building with three investors. They titled the property in their own names as tenants in common, a ridiculously unsafe way to title a multi-owner property. A top Miami law firm represented them but never suggested a safer way to title the building. I see this lack of professional awareness and competence everyday. It's sad.

Even when financial danger is apparent, few lawyers try to protect their clients' wealth before their client loses the lawsuit. It's shocking how many clients think about protecting their assets only when they're about to lose them. Why didn't they and their lawyers protect the assets before the case reached this point?

The greater danger to your wealth is not necessarily the adversary, but your own professional advisor. You are indeed one of the fortunate few when your professional advisor makes asset protection an important part of your financial planning.

Why don't lawyers better protect their clients' assets?

One reason is that few law schools teach asset protection. They excel at teaching budding lawyers how to sue. So graduating lawyers are neither sensitized to the need for asset protection nor know much about it. At least, that's my observation.

I have recommended asset protection courses at the three universities I attended, but so far no luck. The need for this training is obvious, but law schools don't see it.

I think lawyers will do a better job as the litigation explosion grows and asset protection becomes a more common concern for them. Fortunately, we are seeing more professional references and seminars on the subject.

Clients, of course, also must accept some blame. Many do not seek professional advice to protect their wealth or ignore their attorney's recommendations until it is too late.

Do you mean a client shouldn't trust his lawyer's asset protection advice?

No. I say you can't *automatically* assume you get good advice from a lawyer. The lawyer may know what he's talking about or know absolutely nothing. That won't necessarily stop the lawyer from believing he or she has the right answers.

Obviously, you can't stereotype lawyers. Some lawyers are quite skilled at asset protection—many, like myself, make it their specialty. Still, even we have to keep up with constant changes in the law to remain effective.

Lawyers who give bad asset protection advice aren't, of course, necessarily bad lawyers. They may be quite expert at another legal specialty, and they should confine themselves to the areas of law where they skilled.

That is the point. Today, law is complex and specialized. If you need asset protection, find an asset protection lawyer, as you would a legal specialist in another field.

You talk about staying current with the newest trends. Do all asset protection lawyers use offshore strategies?

No. I think too many American lawyers still rely solely on domestic (U.S.-based) planning for asset protection. That's unfortunate, because you get considerably safer protection offshore.

Offshore is a "cutting edge" strategy in asset protection, as lasers are in surgery. But, as in medicine, not all lawyers adapt with the times.

Asset protection, particularly for wealthier clients, usually requires both domestic and offshore strategies. The domestic plan shelters U.S.-based assets—such as real estate. Offshore structures protect nest egg investments. We usually blend the two for the most effective overall protection. A good asset protection lawyer has expertise with both domestic and offshore strategies. A lawyer unfamiliar with offshore planning shortchanges his client.

What are the characteristics of a good asset protection plan? How do you distinguish a good plan from a poor one?

I think there are six essentials for a good wealth protection plan:

First, your plan must protect your *entire* wealth. People frequently overlook assets which remain exposed.

Second, the plan must be legal. As with anything, you can do it right or wrong. Correctly designed, your plan will be perfectly legal and defensible.

Third, asset protection must mesh with your three other financial objectives: Estate planning, investing, and tax planning.

Fourth, your plan must be economical and not overly complicated.

Fifth, you must be psychologically comfortable with your plan.

Sixth, and most importantly, your plan must work. That's the acid test. If you lose your assets to a creditor, the plan failed.

Let's consider each point. You say the plan must protect all assets. Isn't that obvious?

Certainly. Still, you can only *partially* protect yourself. You may overlook intangible assets such as copyrights, patents, contract rights, etc. Or you may believe certain assets are already protected. IRAs are an example. You must also look ahead to protect future or anticipated assets, such as inheritances. Finally, prior asset transfers may be recoverable by creditors as fraudulent conveyances. People can also protect assets under their ownership, but a spouse or children may lose it. A good asset protection plan must also extend protection to those who inherit your assets.

When is asset protection illegal?

One common mistake is to conceal or hide assets. A legitimate asset protection plan never relies upon secrecy, because a judgment creditor can make you disclose your assets. If you answer untruthfully, it is perjury. If you falsify bankruptcy schedules, you are criminally liable for bankruptcy fraud.

You can be truthful when you are confident the creditor can't seize the assets you do disclose.

You can also easily run afoul of money laundering and obstruction of justice laws, particularly when the federal government is the claimant or the assets are connected to illegal activity. That requires us and other asset protection professionals to undertake a "due diligence" on our client's background. We are not in the business of perpetuating crime.

Ideally, asset protection should fit well with your other financial objectives, but don't you sometimes sacrifice other financial goals to gain asset protection?

Not if you coordinate your plan intelligently and before trouble strikes. You can then easily integrate asset protection into a comprehensive financial program. Asset protection planning generally improves upon an estate plan, saves or defers income and estate taxes, and frequently leads our client to better investments.

Our clients frequently report their asset protection program was "unused insurance." They were never sued. Nevertheless, their plan reduced taxes, created a superior estate plan, or introduced them to foreign investments that outperform their domestic investments. These secondary benefits from asset protection are important.

If you attempt to protect yourself *after* trouble strikes, you may jeopardize these other financial goals to prioritize protection, as you have fewer options.

Clients are obviously concerned about fees. What does it cost for good asset protection?

Asset protection is not a cost; it is an investment and must be viewed that way.

Of course, it's impossible to generalize on fees which depend on so many factors: the assets, potential liabilities, state laws, ancillary services (such as estate planning), scope and level of protection, the experience and skill of the practitioner, and many other considerations.

Our average client "invests" several thousand dollars for a good domestic asset protection plan, which includes basic estate planning. Offshore arrangements can add $5,000 to $15,000. Clients with substantial wealth and complex plans spend considerably more, and fees of $50,000 or more are not uncommon.It can also cost $500 to several thousand dollars a year to maintain the asset protection structures.

A good wealth preservation lawyer won't recommend an unnecessarily complicated or costly plan. You can frequently create a strong plan with little or no expense and without a lawyer. The more expensive plan isn't necessarily the better plan.

There are several questions concerning the "effectiveness" of asset protection. Does asset protection really work?

Asset protection works if implemented *before* you have a creditor, and if you design and implement your plan correctly.

But to more fully answer your question, you must understand that asset protection success is also relative.

You can't always be assured you won't lose some assets in certain situations. Or you may settle with a creditor because it's the practical alternative to more costly, time consuming, aggravating and uncertain litigation, even when you are well protected.

We evaluate the success of our plans based on what the client would have lost had we not protected his assets. Ultimately, we ask whether another strategy would have been more effective. When we conclude our client came out better than under any other possible scenario, we did our job.

Can you give us a quick overview of how assets become protected?

You essentially have two strategies:

- Title assets so that they can't be claimed by a creditor.

- Encumber or "equity strip" the asset so it has no value to the creditor.

For the most solid protection, we usually merge both strategies. Everything our client owns is titled in protective entities and also fully encumbered so they become worthless to a creditor, even if the creditor successfully pierced the entity and claimed the asset.

Is it too late to protect yourself once there is a claim against you?

When you have a present or foreseeable creditor, you must concern yourself with the fraudulent transfer or fraudulent conveyance laws.

Summarily, these laws say that if you have a present creditor and transfer assets for less than fair value, with the effect of depriving the creditor payment, the creditor can recover the transferred asset or pursue alternate remedies. Fraudulent transfers are a remedy, not a crime, although in some states they are misdemeanors.

There are considerable cases on fraudulent transfers, and what is permissible is frequently murky. An experienced attorney must review contemplated transfers to see that they are not recoverable by the creditor as a fraudulent transfer. When a creditor can challenge a transfer as fraudulent as a matter of law, and is likely to as a matter of practicality, you have a faulty plan.

To protect assets, why can't you simply title assets with a spouse, friend, or relative as a "straw" with an "asset return" arrangement?

This is always bad planning. Consider the pitfalls. First, your friend or relative may be untrustworthy and double-cross you. Second, your assets are now vulnerable to your "straw's" creditors. Third, these transfers can be set aside as fraudulent by existing creditors. Fourth, there can be serious gift, income and estate tax consequences. Fifth, you lose control and possibly use of the asset. Finally, such arrangements can constitute bankruptcy fraud or illegal concealment. You avoid these potential problems with good asset protection planning.

Can a *future* creditor recover a previous transfer as a fraudulent conveyance?

Under U.S. fraudulent conveyance laws, both present and *future* creditors who could reasonably be foreseen as creditors at the time of the transfer can recover fraudulently transferred assets.

One major problem with U.S. fraudulent conveyance law is that you can't easily predict whether a court will find a particular transfer fraudulent. These laws are vague, and case outcomes frequently are uncertain. That's why *offshore* asset protection is so important. Foreign fraudulent transfers laws are far more precise and predictable than U.S. laws. The asset protection havens are also considerably more protective of debtors. Finally, it is procedurally and substantively more difficult for creditors to recover a fraudulent transfer offshore.

Can you protect your wealth offshore if you already have a claim against you?

Offshore protection is your *safest* alternative once somebody is after you. U.S.-based asset protection is then too unsafe because fraudulent transfers to domestic entities are easily recoverable by creditors through the U.S. courts. It may also be a fraudulent transfer to shelter your money offshore under these same circumstances. Nevertheless, a creditor cannot as readily recover your offshore assets because he no longer can enforce his rights through the U.S. courts. The creditor's rights have not changed, but his power to enforce those rights has greatly diminished. However, never transfer assets offshore to avoid existing claims *without* consulting an attorney experienced in asset protection, because there can be serious consequences.

Before we go too far in our discussion, what is an "offshore haven"?

"Offshore haven" is synonymous with "money haven" or "financial center," which is *any* country with a friendlier financial climate than your own. More simply, an offshore haven is any foreign jurisdiction where your assets or income enjoy *more* protection and/or privacy and/or fewer taxes. A financial haven can also make it easier to conduct business, invest, raise capital, or achieve other important objectives.

What assets can be protected offshore?

You can protect *any* asset; however, liquid, portable assets—cash, securities, and collectibles such as gold or jewelry—are most easily protected because they can be physically relocated outside the United States. Real estate and other onshore possessions, such as a car, boat, or U.S. securities, necessarily remain within U.S. jurisdiction and can be recovered through the U.S. courts if fraudulently conveyed, even to an offshore entity. Your trustees, protectors and fiduciaries, as well as your assets, must be foreign-based to remain beyond the control and recovery powers of American courts.

You can effectively shift your entire wealth from the U.S. to an offshore haven. One way to protect U.S.-based assets is to mortgage or sell the asset and expatriate the cash proceeds offshore. The creditor's only recourse through the U.S. courts is then to seize equity-stripped assets which, obviously, is without value to the creditor.

How do you transfer assets offshore?

It is as simple a process as transferring assets to a domestic entity. You wire transfer funds. Your stockbroker can transfer securities. You transfer personal property by bill of sale or assignment, and convey real estate by deed.

Why is offshore asset protection superior to domestic asset protection?

If you have no present or anticipated claims against you, then a domestic asset protection plan may be adequate. You have many options:

- State homestead laws may protect some home equity.

- You may convert unprotected investments to exempt or protected investments. Annuities and insurance, for instance, are sometimes protected by state law. Retirement accounts may also be partly or fully protected.

- Corporations and limited liability companies can help to shelter assets from creditors.

- Domestic irrevocable trusts can protect assets, although revocable trusts and living trusts do not.

- Husbands and wives in many states may own property together as tenants-by-the-entirety. This protects the property against one spouse's creditors.

- You may mortgage or "equity-strip" property leaving creditors no equity to seize.

- Family limited partnerships are very popular for asset protection because you can control the partnership assets while protecting them and your partnership interest from your personal creditors. I prepare hundreds of FLPs each year as the foundation for my domestic asset protection program.

This only scratches the surface. There are many ways to protect wealth within the U.S. Still, domestic asset protection has restrictions and limitations, particularly when you have existing creditors.

What portion of your assets should you protect offshore?

If your primary goal is asset protection, then invest offshore as much of your wealth as possible. If asset protection is not your immediate concern, invest your nest egg funds or wealth reserved for your retirement and not foreseeably needed for living expenses. Through direct transfers and "equity stripping," you protect virtually all your wealth offshore. This should be your goal against serious financial dangers.

Who typically seeks offshore financial protection?

People from every background, but mostly high-risk professionals, entrepreneurs, and business owners. Physicians, lawyers, developers, real estate owners, and corporate officers and directors lead the list. We also frequently protect business assets offshore. Many of our U.S. business owner clients also find legitimate tax advantages offshore.

Some people start slowly with their offshore wealth protection, investing perhaps $20,000 or less. They transfer more wealth offshore as their confidence, resources or need for protection increases.

The speaker at one asset protection seminar suggested that a limited partnership adequately protects assets and that offshore protection is unnecessary. Do you agree?

I agree the limited partnership is a good protective structure, but it has limitations.

First, an FLP cannot own S corporation shares or your family home without losing tax benefits. These assets can be owned by an offshore trust.

Second, creditors can recover fraudulent transfers to a limited partnership. It is extremely difficult to overturn offshore transfers under the same circumstances.

An LP is a superior structure to protect domestic or U.S. based assets, and we set up quite a few; still, "results-oriented" judges can ignore the law and create convenient theories to pierce LP protection.

When you have significant wealth or serious problems, why gamble with uncertain protection? You immeasurably improve protection offshore.

How do offshore havens protect assets from lawsuits and creditors? Why are they such powerful wealth protectors?

First, good asset protection countries neither recognize nor enforce U.S. judgments or judicial or administrative orders—such as from the IRS. You thus enjoy complete jurisdictional immunity.

Countries that enforce American judgments or court orders are worthless for asset protection. Some countries partly cooperate with American law enforcement, whether through treaty, such as Mutual Legal Assistance Treaties (MLAT), or through "comity," a reciprocal recognition of the judicial decrees of another country. Very few countries completely ignore the legal orders of another country. But certain countries will not enforce U.S. *civil* decrees. These are the countries we use.

Because a haven won't recognize an American civil decree, the creditor must re-litigate its case within the haven. This may be impractical or impossible if the statute of limitations for commencing suit has expired. These havens have other procedural obstacles to block litigation. Asset protection havens are debtor-oriented and strive hard to protect because protection is what they sell.

Asset protection havens also have special laws that allow debtors to set up protective structures within their country, including ordinances for establishing offshore asset protection trusts, limited liability companies, limited partnerships, foundations, captive insurance companies or comparable entities that are considerably more protective than U.S. entities.

Finally, asset protection havens are also good privacy havens (but privacy havens are not necessarily asset protection havens).

How much money is protected offshore?

Nobody really knows because so much money secretively moves in and out of the many financial centers. About $8 trillion is estimated to be internationally invested. Americans lead the offshore trend because we have the greatest unrest concerning the safety of our wealth and the unrestricted opportunity to move money offshore. Only four countries have lenient foreign exchange rules. America, the largest, has an estimated $4 trillion invested offshore. Expatriating funds is a rapidly increasing trend. Each year more wealth leaves America and other high-tax, over-regulated, and litigious countries.

The question is what will their governments and ours do to stop this capital flight . . . and when?

What features are most important when selecting an offshore haven?

You can consider many possible factors, but five are most important:

1) Strong asset protection legislation.

2) A predictable legal system.

3) No or low taxes.

4) Laws to protect privacy and confidentiality.

5) No exchange controls.

The criteria will change as your objectives change. You must match your reasons for going offshore to the haven that can best satisfy those needs. For asset protection, the most important criteria is the haven's ability and willingness to protect assets. Everything else is secondary.

What features are most important for asset protection?

About twenty havens provide some level of asset protection, yet only a few are very protective on these points:

- *Statute of Limitations*: The shortest time to challenge fraudulent transfers. Only when you reach this date are prior transfers safe. The statutes of limitations range from unlimited duration to a brief one year, which, of course, is most favorable.

- *Non-recognition of foreign judgments*: The haven must neither recognize nor enforce foreign judgments. The creditor must be forced to re-litigate the case in the haven.

- *Burden of proof on fraudulent intent*: A creditor who pursues an alleged fraudulent transfer must prove the transfer was made with fraudulent intent. The debtor should not be required to prove the opposite.

- *Standard of proof*: The standard of proof on fraudulent intent should be rigid. Some havens require the creditor to establish fraud by a mere preponderance of the evidence, as in civil cases. Others demand fraud proven beyond a reasonable doubt, which is far more difficult.

• *Ability to freeze assets*: The haven must not allow a creditor to attach or restrain assets before judgment.

• *Invalidity of fraudulent transfers or subsequent creditors*: The haven must protect assets transferred before the liability, notwithstanding subsequent fraudulent transfers.

• *Clear differentiation of creditors*: Their laws should clearly distinguish between present creditors who can pursue fraudulent conveyances and future creditors who cannot.

• *Conditions precedent to litigation*: The haven should impose procedural obstacles to litigation. For instance, must the creditor post a significant cash bond before litigating? Must the creditor retain counsel from within the haven? Are contingent fees prohibited? These and other procedural restraints greatly discourage creditor claims.

- *Forced heirship override provisions*: Can a trust grantor exclude a wife or child from inheriting his assets? Other laws enhance asset protection, and some features and laws are quite novel. The many possible asset protection features explain why asset protection lawyers differ in their preferences when selecting a haven.

There are other features to consider when choosing any haven:

- Limitations on monetary accumulations.

- Statutes on perpetuities or compulsory termination date for the trust or entity.

- Restrictions on corporate trustees.

- Restrictions on protectors.

- Governmental and private fees. Allowance of other trusts (such as charitable remainder, insurance, or children's trusts).

- Governmental controls over the trust.

- Recordings of trust requirements.

- Grantor residency requirements.

- Registration requirements.

- Trustee residency requirements.

- Protector residency requirements.

- MLAT and other treaties.

- Communications and transportation.

- Banking availability.

- Adequacy of professional services.

How important is the country's economic and political stability?

Economic and political stability is relatively unimportant compared to their legal protection, because you usually do not invest within the haven. Of course, your haven must be politically stable so you are confident with their laws and enforcement policies. However, should the country become politically or economically unstable, you can quickly move your assets to a more secure haven. You essentially shop for "laws," not economic or political climate.

How important is good banking, communication and transportation?

You can find quality banks virtually in every haven. You will need a financially-sound, good service bank without branches in the United States. You can bank outside the haven, so banking is not ordinarily important in selecting a haven.

Transportation and communication are even less important. Few Americans have reason to journey to the country where their money is protected. Communication is more important, but every haven has adequate communication systems today.

What countries are offshore havens?

Offshore havens of every size, variety and political persuasion are throughout the world. Bermuda, the British Virgin Islands, and the Bahamas hug America's southeast coast. The Cayman Islands, Turks and Caicos, Nevis, and Antigua dot the Caribbean. The Isle of Man and Channel Islands—Jersey and Guernsey—shadow England. Switzerland, Liechtenstein, Luxembourg, Hungary, and Austria are key European havens. The Philippines, Singapore and Hong Kong serve the Pacific Rim. Cyprus, Malta, and Gibraltar are Mediterranean havens. The Cook Islands are near New Zealand.

Protective havens cluster near industrialized countries whose arcane laws force their wealthier citizens to find friendlier places for their money. But the world is shrinking quickly and the choice of haven no longer depends upon geography, because you can now easily invest wherever you can best satisfy your financial objectives. Electronic banking makes it as fast and easy to bank in another hemisphere as next door.

Offshore stars rise and fall quickly. New, more competitive havens constantly emerge. Gibraltar, the Cook Islands, Nevis, the Marianas, Belize, Seychelles, Vanuatu, the Turks and Caicos, and Montserrat are more recent offshore contenders. St. Vincent is an emerging haven. Other bright stars are on the horizon.

Newer havens usually have more advantageous laws to gain an edge over older havens. Offshore centers seldom attract foreign money by chance. They strategically, creatively, and competitively restructure their laws to become more protective and financially attractive.

For each rising star, another loses its glow. For centuries, Switzerland was the premier secret banking capital, yet Switzerland's privacy has greatly eroded largely due to international (mostly United States) economic and political pressures. The Caymans has become overly-controlled by the U.S. Several smaller, more recent upstarts offer considerably better privacy and protection because they have thus far avoided international pressures to compromise their protection. These havens are rising stars. Nevis is a good example.

The British Crown Colonies were the earliest havens. England itself is a key financial center but is not a haven, chiefly because of its many foreign treaties, absence of protective laws, and high taxes. But it's still quite different with some British Commonwealth countries: the Caymans, British Virgin Islands, Bermuda, Turks and Caicos, Gibraltar, and Malta. As independent countries, they have sufficient political and legal autonomy and enact their own tax, privacy, asset protection, and banking laws. Their United Kingdom affiliation provides them economic and political stability, but also vulnerability to potential pressure from England. Nothing is constant in this business.

Whatever their size, history, or geography, every offshore haven has laws and banking practices that in a variety of ways can more effectively protect your wealth. They differ only in their methods and successes in achieving these goals.

What mistakes are most common when selecting an offshore haven?

First, don't accept a haven's aggressive marketing claims at face value. Offshore havens are fiercely competitive and their promotional materials can convincingly portray illusive advantages. Carefully investigate a haven's laws and practices, and never rely on their past reputation or popularity.

You must know what features are most important to you and whether the protection you need will be there when you need it. You cannot take this for granted. As a post-doctoral research scholar at the

London School of Economics, I thoroughly researched how the various offshore trust havens perform in practice. From this study, I found that promises and practice can be quite different.

Another mistake is to believe one haven or protective entity is always best. This is no more sensible than believing that one house or car is ideal for everyone. Yet, some offshore lawyers use "cookie-cutter" arrangements because it is easiest. What is right for one client may be wrong for another.

How does the IRS view offshore investing?

The IRS wants American money kept in the U.S. so they can better monitor income reporting. This should come as no surprise.

There are only a few instances where U.S. taxpayers can legally avoid or defer income, capital gains, or estate taxes. Still, offshore tax savings are touted by some unscrupulous offshore promoters. While you can gain many benefits offshore, saving taxes is seldom a benefit. You will need an advisor familiar with international tax laws to decide if the few remaining legitimate offshore tax advantages can apply to you. The rule of thumb: don't go offshore if saving taxes is your primary goal.

I can tell you that protecting your wealth offshore won't increase your chances for an audit. If you properly report your offshore income and investments you will have no difficulty with the IRS. Remember—it is perfectly legal to go offshore with your money.

2

OFFSHORE FINANCIAL PRIVACY

Dr. Goldstein, why is financial privacy so important?

Most people don't want snoops probing their financial affairs, so they keep their money offshore for privacy. Strict offshore secrecy laws completely shield your financial affairs from an inquisitive government, creditors, competitors, ex-spouses, and others who may be curious about your wealth. Your financial affairs in America are public. You can't fully appreciate offshore secrecy until you suffer the indignity of a stranger or adversary uncovering all your financial and private affairs, which is an everyday ritual in America and in most major countries where privacy has vanished.

Whatever little privacy we still have will soon be completely obliterated through newer invasive technologies and increased governmental demands to monitor our every financial transaction. Who wants to live in a fishbowl?

Why hide information, unless it points to something illegal?

Most Americans with offshore wealth have legitimate reasons for financial secrecy. Business, competitors, relatives, litigation or estate planning situations demand privacy. Washington D.C. neither respects nor guarantees privacy. Our laws force you to expose your finances to any litigant, creditor, tax collector, ex-spouse, prospective heir, competitor, business associate or other curiosity seeker. National security, drug control, and crime prevention are lame excuses for Washington D.C. destroying our financial privacy. Our predatory society makes it more important to become financially invisible, but our government makes it impossible.

Why must Americans seeking offshore financial privacy justify their motives? They shouldn't.

Your assets may never be threatened. You may never be sued. The government may never be keenly interested in you. Nevertheless, you may want confidentiality for countless personal reasons. Your investments may carry political overtones. Past financial dealings can hurt your reputation or career. Visible wealth may attract swindlers, gold-diggers, litigants, ne'er-do-well family members, shady promoters, and other parasites and vultures that populate our society. Why *not* keep your affairs private?

How easily can someone discover your assets?

For about $500 I can find out nearly everything about your finances. High-powered computers and vanished privacy rights can give anyone a quick fix on your wealth. Public records reveal mountains of information about you. Private asset locators expose personal or business assets for a plaintiff's lawyers, creditors, and our own government—anyone who will pay their small fee.

Beyond losing our privacy, our government has created a massive spy system. forcing every bank to screen millions of daily electronic funds transfers for suspicious or unusual activity. The IRS is now wired to every bank and most state and local agencies. The FBI has the power to seize records or phones without a warrant. These things are happening in America right now. That's why privacy-seekers want their money offshore.

How strict are offshore secrecy laws?

Offshore bank secrecy laws protect all banking or financial records against disclosure—whether to governments or private parties. Their blocking statutes prohibit the disclosure, copying, inspection or removal of documents, even under a foreign court order. This prevents the deposition or subpoena of witnesses within the haven.

You enjoy complete financial privacy in a strong secrecy haven. They protect bank records, books, records and correspondence between yourself and your professional advisors, and communications and transactions with common carriers, agents, employees, directors, customers, and others directly or indirectly involved with your offshore finances.

Offshore secrecy laws in good privacy havens are strictly enforced. Offshore banks cannot violate their secrecy laws, regardless of circumstances, and these havens harshly penalize secrecy-law violators with imprisonment for ten or more years. Offshore bankers who snitch on their depositors go to jail. The U.S. jails bankers who do *not* snitch on their depositors. It's an interesting contrast.

Which havens are best for secrecy?

The best European privacy havens are Liechtenstein, Luxembourg, and Austria. The Bahamas, Nevis, and Cook Islands have excellent secrecy and asset protection laws.

The British Virgin Islands, Bermuda, Caymans, Turks and Caicos, Antigua, Belize, Gibraltar, Isle of Man, and Jersey, once good privacy havens, are now under great pressure from the U.S. and England to open their records and tax foreign capital. Their future is too shaky.

Offshore secrecy havens succumb to international, legal or political pressures. Countries that rely heavily on U.S. financial support are always a poor choice when privacy is your objective, and you must objectively evaluate treaty impacts on a haven's privacy. Secrecy is comparative. You must constantly compare secrecy standards and practices in our fast-moving world where laws, treaties, and international relationships change rapidly. Mutual Legal Assistance Treaties (MLATs) were originally designed to target non-tax crimes but have become a lever for the United States to extract tax information concerning Americans.

Switzerland, for example, supposedly drops secrecy only under circumstances carefully prescribed in their treaty with the United States, which does not include tax evasion. But American prosecutors readily obtain financial information from Swiss banks under the mere allegation of a treaty crime. Merely alleging a drug law violation routinely uncovers tax evasion records.

Avoid MLAT havens if you can, but you may eventually run out of such havens. The United States, like an overgrown octopus, stretches its tentacles of influence globally. Few countries can resist. For privacy, select that rare haven that refuses to go to bed with Uncle Sam.

In practice, how do offshore banks insure secrecy for their depositors?

Start by contrasting how American banks operate. American banks must relinquish subpoenaed records. Offshore records, on the other hand, are fully protected from court orders and subpoenas because your offshore bank cannot legally divulge financial information about you to anyone, except under treaty provisions.

Offshore banks are also jurisdictionally immune to service of process which effectively bars writs of execution or attachment orders. Secrecy laws not only protect entrusted funds from creditor seizure on domestic judgments, but also protect the confidentiality of banking records. Whether it is a civil lawsuit or criminal investigation, offshore banks cannot disclose protected information.

If an offshore bank has no presence within the U.S. (via American-based branches or affiliates), it is beyond the jurisdiction of American courts. American courts also bar information demands if disclosure violates the haven's secrecy laws, even if the offshore bank is owned or operated by U.S. residents. The offshore bank, as a separate entity, is obligated to protect depositor confidentiality. Secrecy laws everywhere prohibit using a bank principal's citizenry to circumvent privacy laws applicable to offshore banks.

In summary, any request or subpoena for bank information will be rejected by the offshore bank. No records can be produced. No bank employee can testify. No bank representative within the haven will be questioned. No government agency or private litigant can compel otherwise. That's privacy!

How safe are foreign banks?

Offshore banking is absolutely safe *if* you bank with larger, more well established banks. Foreign banks have fewer failures than American banks. However, they have no depositor insurance, so select a financially-sound bank so your money is safe. Our office publishes a list of financially-sound banks in all privacy havens, or check *Polks Directory of International Banks*, available at most libraries.

Dr. Goldstein, at one of your seminars you commented that to maintain privacy you must separate your offshore finances from your U.S. finances. Please explain.

For offshore financial privacy, you must create two entirely separate financial worlds. Your *public* world is your home country; where you work, pay taxes, keep your bank accounts and other investments and financial matters that the world will know about.

Your *private* world is offshore, where you keep your "invisible" money: funds and other investments that only you, close family members, tax agencies (if applicable), and your offshore professionals know about. This private world shelters your major bank accounts, investments, business interests, and other nest egg assets.

Separate your private and public worlds. Avoid direct transactions between your onshore (public world) bank and offshore (private world) bank. You compromise secrecy when expatriated money is too easily traced. Indirectly transfer funds through one or more intermediaries. An offshore company can be an intermediary for redeposit to your offshore account.

Money deposited to one offshore haven can secretly go to other offshore accounts. You sacrifice privacy *only* when one haven is not secretive. To secretly repatriate funds, you reverse the process. Funds repatriated to the United States can be wired through offshore intermediaries.

How do you transfer money offshore?

Most Americans moving money offshore don't try to conceal it. They only want their finances secret once offshore. You may want to secretly transfer funds offshore believing secrecy provides asset protection, which is untrue. You gain protection through the haven's protective laws and the structure that now owns your assets. Offshore assets are no less protected because creditors know about them, nor can you legally conceal offshore assets if a creditor compels disclosure under oath.

Wire transfers are most commonly used to transfer funds offshore. You can also legally send a check or money order for any amount offshore, however, banks microfilm all checks and wire transfers. Most offshore banks wire transfer funds to correspondent banks or foreign exchange dealers in the United States and wire transfers are completed within 48 hours.

Personally transporting money offshore is expensive and inconvenient, but an alternative if your haven can double as a vacation spot. You can transfer $10,000 offshore in cash, travelers checks, or other bearer currency, but amounts above this must be reported to U.S. Customs, who can disclose this to the IRS and other federal agencies, but not private parties.

You can also personally transport precious commodities: diamonds, rare coins, or gold, and convert them offshore to funds for deposit.

Can a creditor force you to disclose your offshore finances?

Yes. And you must then truthfully disclose what *you know*, including the funds transferred offshore, their source, and presently-known investments. However, when you have creditors, your trustee may switch investments to those you do not know about, creating a "blind" trust. Creditors cannot then discover your *present* offshore assets through your disclosure; however, this is only an added precaution. Creditors have little recourse against properly disclosed protected offshore investments.

U.S. citizens with foreign bank accounts of $10,000 or more must report them to the IRS. Doesn't this destroy privacy?

You are exempt from reporting an offshore account if you have neither signing authority nor control over the account, or no interest as a beneficiary. Americans with signing authority—including trustees and protectors—must report offshore accounts although they have no beneficial or direct financial interest in the account. I advise my clients to check the box disclosing offshore accounts whenever there is a question. Disclosure will not trigger an audit.

The forms you must file with the Treasury Department are non-IRS forms, not considered tax information and not subject to IRS Code restrictions that limit disclosure of return information.

IRS and Treasury Department reporting requirements can be complex. Review the offshore reporting requirements at least annually with your attorney and/or tax advisor, who can inform you of more recent reporting regulations. Don't let IRS reporting intimidate you. Reporting will not cause tax problems, but failure to report may.

For protection, why can't I simply hide my money in a privacy haven bank account?

Many people do, but it's very poor protection. A judgment creditor (or IRS) can make you disclose offshore assets. If you lie to conceal them, you commit perjury. Once they are disclosed, a U.S. court can order you to repatriate the unprotected money for the benefit of the creditor. A foreign bank account is not creditor-protected, because the account remains under your control, and you can comply with a court's repatriation and turnover order under threat of contempt.

Dr. Goldstein, how would you title assets offshore for maximum lawsuit protection?

You have several alternatives. Of course, titling foreign assets in your own name offers no protection, because a U.S. court can compel you to repatriate these assets.

An IBC (foreign company) protects you only slightly more because a U.S. court will logically conclude that you are the true owner of any offshore company that you funded and then give the creditor your offshore company, or order you to repatriate its assets.

For protection, use an entity that provides true protection, not illusory protection. Some options:

- The offshore trust (or Foreign Asset Protection Trust ("FAPT")

- Nevis LLC (or a similar entity, such as a Bahamian limited partnership)

- Private foundations

- Hybrid companies or companies limited by guarantee.

OFFSHORE
TRUSTS

Which asset protection entities are most popular?

The offshore asset protection trust is the most common, because the trust was the only protective offshore structure until recently.

In most situations, the offshore trust is still a popular and good choice; however, newer protective entities are gaining popularity because of their advantages over the trust.

Since the trust is most frequently used, let's start there. What is an offshore trust?

An offshore asset protection trust is a special trust established in a foreign country with strict laws that protect trust assets from lawsuits and creditors. The trust is secretive and also provides an entity for international investing.

This trust is known by several other names: Creditor Protection Trust, Offshore Trust, International Trust, Asset Conservation Trust, Foreign Trust, or Grantor Trust.

The offshore trust is a relatively new twist to the trust's long heritage. Only since the 1980's have certain foreign countries enacted special asset protection trust laws. While most offshore trusts have been established this decade, it is now one of the most popular trusts, rising in popularity with the need and demand for asset protection.

Can an offshore trust be used for purposes other than creditor protection?

Yes. We frequently set up offshore trusts for:

- forced heirship law avoidance

- premarital planning

- estate planning

- Medicaid planning and entitlement preservation

- international business planning

- regulatory avoidance

How does an offshore trust compare to an irrevocable U.S. Trust?

The offshore trust is similar to the domestic irrevocable trust, but provides greater protection.

Most importantly, the offshore trust is established in a foreign haven. That difference is critical. Irrevocable U.S. trusts are vulnerable to attacks by the grantor's existing creditors through creditor-friendly U.S. courts.

The offshore trust has other protective features:

- *Foreign law governs.* The debtor-friendly laws of the trust haven govern its enforcement.

- *Anti-duress provisions.* If a U.S. court compels the grantor to repatriate trust assets, the trustee must refuse this demand.

- *Flight provisions.* Authorizes the trustee to relocate trust assets to another trust haven if the trust became endangered in its present haven.

- *Discretionary powers.* The trustee decides such issues, as distributions to beneficiaries.

- *Provisions to alter or terminate beneficial rights.* The trustee can alter the rights of any beneficiary under creditor attack to eliminate or frustrate creditor claims against the trust.

In what countries can you establish offshore trusts?

About twenty offshore havens have trust legislation. Americans most frequently use Nevis, the Caymans, Bahamas, Belize, Cook Islands, and Turks and Caicos, but there are other excellent trust havens. Jersey and the Isle of Man, for instance, attract money from the United Kingdom. Geography has historically influenced popularity, but this is changing with modern telecommunication.

Who are the parties to the Trust?

The Trust has four parties:

- *The grantor* (or the settlor, donor or trustor) creates and funds the trust, appoints the initial trustees and protector and names the beneficiaries.

- *The trustee* manages the trust for the benefit of the beneficiaries.

- *The beneficiaries* receive the trust's income and/or assets.

- *A protector* oversees the trustee.

Who can be the grantor?

Any adult or legal entity can, as the grantor, create and fund the trust. Parents or grandparents frequently create trusts to protect their wealth for their children or grandchildren. Husbands and wives as co-grantors combine their wealth into one trust, or establish separate trusts. Who becomes the grantor usually depends upon complex tax, asset protection, estate planning, business, and personal considerations.

For confidentiality, an offshore corporation or foreign lawyer can establish the trust as the nominee grantor. Many offshore trusts do not name the grantor, and in some jurisdictions you need not record the trust which also protects grantor identity. A grantor must have the legal capacity, authority, and intent to form the trust.

Selecting the appropriate grantor is important, because the trustee is ultimately guided by the grantor's wishes, to the exclusion, for instance, of a non-grantor spouse. Determining the proper grantor is a point to discuss with your attorney.

What powers does the trustee have and how can I be certain the trustee won't steal my money?

The trust gives the trustee the powers to do whatever is needed to protect or enhance the trust assets. These powers, found in any irrevocable trust, include the right to sell, buy, lease, encumber or invest trust assets, defend or prosecute claims, pay debts and taxes, hire other professionals, make loans, and/or distribute income or principal to beneficiaries.

The Trust purposely grants the trustee broad powers and the grantor no or negligible authority. The grantor who has more control loses asset protection. Delegating control over your wealth to a foreign trustee will be less frightening once you realize trustees readily comply with a grantor's appropriate and voluntary wishes concerning the trust.

A grantor concerned about losing control can, through a number of strategies, balance asset protection against the desire to retain control; however, your attorney must ultimately decide what control you can safely retain without jeopardizing asset protection.

If delegating complete control to the trustee concerns you, consider several options: Appoint a protector who will follow your directions. Since the protector can replace the trustee, you gain *alter ego* control. Or make the trust *revocable* until a specified event— such as a creditor lawsuit—when the trust automatically becomes irrevocable. You can also establish a limited partnership owned by the trust as its limited partner. As the general partner, you control partnership assets in the U.S. until under legal duress when the partnership assets can be transferred to the trust. You can also become the managing director of an IBC (foreign company) owned and funded by the trust. Another alternative is to control the trusteeship until threatened by creditors. You, your spouse, or another U.S. designee can be co-trustees with your foreign trustee. Moreover, your protector can co-sign trust accounts. You can also keep your trust unfunded until necessary for asset protection. There are other control-retention techniques.

Other safeguards can insure that your assets will be handled as you wish. Concern is natural when a stranger on another continent fully controls *your* money. You question whether the trustee will embezzle, squander or lose your money on bad investments. Fortunately, there is little cause for concern. Foreign trustees have an impeccable record for honesty and prudence. As professionals, they are usually fully bonded, licensed, and backed by the reputation of their own countries. No offshore haven can afford an embezzlement scandal. The trustee's haven would likely make restitution for the dishonesty of one of their trustees, although there are few reported cases of trustee embezzlement or dishonesty.

Can you be a trustee or protector of your own trust or control the trust?

For maximum protection, you should be neither the trustee nor protector of your own trust. Relinquish control of the trust to foreign-based trustees and protectors beyond the jurisdiction of U.S. courts.

Trusts protect assets only when the grantor surrenders control over the trust assets to the trustee. The trustee cannot be a mere alter-ego or sham for the grantor. This is the trade-off for asset protection.

You will resist losing control or decision-making authority and want more control without realizing you then forfeit protection. Creditors scrutinize trust arrangements and courts set aside sham transactions that create illusory rights not intended to have legal effect.

Creditors through their wide discovery powers, can unravel a trust if they show that the grantor or beneficiaries made trust decisions. If the court concludes the trustee is merely the grantor's *alter ego*, the court will declare the trust a legal fiction and dissolve it for the benefit of the grantor's creditors. You can make *requests* to your trustee, but not *command* or do the trustee's job. Violate this sacred rule and you jeopardize protection.

How do I find and select a good trustee?

There are excellent trustees in every offshore trust haven. They are usually lawyers or chartered accountants who passed rigid licensing examinations.

Your trustee should administer many trusts and other offshore entities. Active trustees provide the widest range of services, are usually bonded, and deliver service most efficiently.

While qualifications are important, you must also be comfortable with your trustee. Test your relationship.

Discuss objectives, investment preferences and financial philosophies. Anticipate special considerations, such as prospective loans from the trust. Don't accept this relationship on faith alone. Your trustee must be cooperative, flexible and responsive to your needs. My clients usually meet several prospective trustees to intelligently compare and choose.

Check trustee references. How many clients do they serve? How satisfied are they? How has their firm grown? Who else within the firm may handle your account? Will you be assigned only one individual to handle your account? Will they provide client references? Bank references? Bonding? Can they deliver all the services you need, such as portfolio management? Are they accessible? Responsive?

Location is important for convenience. You will seldom meet personally with your trustee, but communication is difficult with a trustee in a time zone 12 hours behind your own.

Choose the right size and type trustee firm. If you are ·more conservative, or have a larger portfolio, you may prefer a major institutional trustee. However, non-institutional trustees have an excellent record and are quite safe. Banks charge higher trustee fees than private trust companies and are less flexible. Most offshore trustees are private trust companies.

Trustee fees are competitive, but compare fees and negotiate lower fees if it will not compromise service.

An attorney with offshore experience can recommend trustees and, of course, I can refer you to trustees who have efficiently served my clients.

What is the role of the trust protector?

The protector essentially prevents misdeeds by the trustee. The protector can only veto trustee decisions or actions that the protector considers inappropriate. The protector cannot force the trustee to act. For example, the trustee may require protector approval for the trustee to sell trust investments or withdraw trust funds. The protector thus ensures the trustee acts in the best interests of the grantor and beneficiaries.

The protector's most important power is the authority to replace the trustee. Through the grantor's authority to appoint initial protectors, and the protector's authority to change trustees, the grantor indirectly asserts some control over the trustee and the trust. Replacement trustees must be independent of the grantor or any beneficiary and not be appointed by any court or on behalf of any or creditor.

You can legally be the protector of your own trust. However, as the protector, a U.S. court may conclude that you control the trust through your power to change trustees, and in that manner can force the repatriation of trust assets to satisfy creditors. For that reason, a grantor should *not* be his own protector. Spouses, other relatives, business associates or professional advisors can be appointed, but a professional foreign protector is recommended for the same reason as foreign trustees. You want your protector beyond the jurisdiction of American courts.

Because the protector oversees the trustee, and greatly influences trust matters, appointing the correct protector requires no less thought than selecting the trustee.

What criteria are most important when selecting a protector?

Since the protector's role is to veto trustee actions and, if necessary, replace the trustee, a good protector must understand how things work offshore and have the time and willingness to oversee the trustee and approve his actions. This may be a friend, business associate, or close relative. The grantor should not be the trust protector or someone he obviously controls. Of course, never select a protector recommended by your trustee. Your protector must be independent. Your attorney can help you locate a professional foreign protector which are frequently firms that also offer trustee and similar fiduciary services.

How do you name beneficiaries?

You select the beneficiaries of an offshore trust as you would under your domestic will or living trust.

With a living trust, you usually name yourself the sole lifetime beneficiary, but a grantor of an offshore trust should not be the only beneficiary for creditor-protection purposes. The grantor, however, can be a co-beneficiary.

Beneficiaries are specifically named or identified by category or class. For example, you may designate as beneficiaries: "all your surviving or future children in equal shares."

The trust specifically excludes adverse parties as potential beneficiaries. Creditors or other parties with an interest adverse to the grantor, the beneficiaries, or the trust generally, cannot be a beneficiary, trustee, or protector, even under court order.

There are many creative ways to use offshore trusts for estate planning and for tax and other legal advantages. Beneficiaries can be natural persons, profit or non-profit corporations, associations, partnerships, other trusts or any other legal entity, whether American or foreign. As the grantor, you designate beneficiaries and can expand, contract, terminate or shift beneficial interests, subject to trustee approval. This is accomplished through a statement of wishes directed to the trustee.

Can the grantor of an offshore trust change beneficiaries or other terms or conditions of distribution?

The grantor can always *request* the trustee, through a side letter (the letter of wishes), to modify lifetime or testamentary beneficiaries or conditions for distribution. However, you can only *request* changes. A trustee ordinarily honors new wishes but is *not obligated* to do so. Trustees won't refuse reasonable requests that do not compromise asset protection, which, of course, is their chief concern.

Is trust secrecy important for protection?

Secrecy does not protect trust assets. That is why the trust is a *legal* alternative if you want creditor protection without *illegally* concealing assets. A creditor who knows about your trust cannot claim its assets. With the trust you can be both *truthful* and *safe*. If you bury your money in a coffee can in your backyard or squirrel money in an offshore bank account, you are safe only if you are *dishonest* about your assets.

How do offshore trusts and other asset protection structures protect against creditors?

Offshore trusts and similar protective entities are necessary today *only* because we have so many lawsuits. It is your big weapon to duel plaintiffs armed with runaway laws, sympathetic juries, and greedy lawyers. The trust discourages litigation three ways:

First, it provides secrecy for your wealth. Second, the trust should convince even the most determined plaintiff it would be difficult, if not impossible, to collect. You thus gain leverage to settle cheaply or discourage lawsuits in the first place. Finally, a judgment creditor could not seize trust assets even if the creditor presses his claim.

An offshore trust protects assets through several mechanisms: First, the trust haven will neither recognize nor enforce U.S. judgments or judicial or administrative orders. You thus enjoy complete jurisdictional immunity. Second, the trust is an irrevocable, discretionary trust. Since the grantor no longer owns or controls the trust assets, the grantor's future creditors have no legal right or access to the trust assets. Third, the trust's many unique anti-duress, anti-creditor provisions will frustrate creditor attempts to pierce the trust or recover trust assets.

Must I immediately fund the offshore trust or can I delay funding the trust until there's a lawsuit?

Many people delay funding their trust until absolutely necessary. You may prefer to continue your U.S. investments or want your money under *your* control until it is no longer safe.

One popular solution is to organize a U.S. limited partnership, with the offshore trust as its 99 percent limited partner. As the general partner, you would manage and control the partnership assets. The partnership assets may never be distributed to the trust nor leave the United States unless threatened; meanwhile, the partnership assets can remain titled to the partnership under your control.

Combining a limited partnership and offshore trust creates formidable protection while you straddle the fence. You may not want your funds offshore *if* a lawsuit can be avoided or resolved. On the other hand, you may need stronger protection than the limited partnership *if* you lose the case or partnership assets are endangered. The assets would then be distributed to the partners. The offshore trust as the limited partner would receive the partnership proceeds offshore, beyond creditor reach.

If assets are fraudulently transferred offshore, can a U.S. court reclaim these trust assets for the creditor?

One advantage of offshore protection over domestic asset protection is that assets fraudulently transferred within the U.S. are recoverable through U.S. courts with continued jurisdiction over these assets. However, an American court has no jurisdiction over offshore assets. Thus, offshore assets are better protected than U.S.-based assets, particularly when they are susceptible to fraudulent transfer claims through our courts.

This point is important. A claim can always be raised from the past, and for asset protection you must withstand a fraudulent transfer claim. Unfortunately, there are few instances where a creditor cannot argue fraudulent conveyance. You avoid this vulnerability and uncertainty with an offshore trust.

Can a court compel the American debtor to repatriate trust funds or face contempt?

A U.S. judge cannot redirect ownership of offshore assets beyond U.S. court jurisdiction; however, an American grantor-debtor *is* under the court's powers. Still, a court *cannot* compel a debtor to do what the debtor has no legal power to do. This emphasizes why trust assets and those who control the trust must be outside the U.S.

An offshore account or offshore company won't protect offshore assets because you *do* directly control your offshore company and personal accounts. A U.S. court *can* then order you to repatriate these funds. To avoid contempt, you must show that offshore fiduciaries control the assets and that you are powerless to repatriate the assets you no longer own or control. Additionally, you must show that you did not establish the trust to frustrate a foreseeable U.S. order. "Self-incapacity" can also be contemptuous. That is why you must protect your wealth offshore as soon as possible.

Can a creditor pursue a fraudulent transfer claim in the trust haven?

Possibly. However, these havens provide enormous debtor protection and impose obstacles few creditors can overcome. One example is their short statute of limitations. Claims usually must be filed within one or two years from transfer. Few creditors can timely challenge an offshore transfer. The creditor also must *prove beyond a reasonable doubt* that it was a fraudulent conveyance, which is very difficult. Nevis requires the creditor to post a sizeable cash bond before commencing litigation and hire local counsel who will work on a fee-only basis. An American creditor with a U.S. judgment must also re-litigate the case within the haven and obtain judgment from the haven before it can set aside the transfer as fraudulent. You cannot re-litigate the case if the claim is not based on the laws of the haven. These many requirements filter most prospective claims. Of course, no respectable asset protection haven can completely disregard creditor fraudulent transfer claims, but they can make it difficult—*exceptionally* difficult—to pursue these claims.

What if a determined creditor tries to set aside the transfer and seize the trust assets?

Your trustee can then relocate your offshore trust assets to another trust in a new asset protection haven and appoint a successor trustee for that trust. The creditor must then begin new legal proceedings in that haven. This "flee" provision is found in most offshore trusts. Creditors tire from a chase when trust assets can continuously be moved to still other havens and structures. The flee provision, or "Cuba clause," is one of the more powerful asset protection provisions of the offshore trust, because it deprives the creditor any practical opportunity to reach offshore trust assets.

Considering their many formidable obstacles, how frequently do creditors attack offshore trusts?

There are fewer than three creditor challenges for every hundred offshore trusts. These rare cases are typically settled advantageously. Without offshore protection, these creditors would have undoubtedly recovered significantly more. The fact that 97 out of 100 creditors *won't* challenge offshore transfers strongly endorses its asset protection powers. In many cases, the creditor had the legal right to recover. There was no attempted recovery because it was impractical. A creditor can spend enormous legal fees and never recover offshore assets, even when the creditor has the legal right. With offshore asset protection, it is usually impractical for a creditor to pursue a claim, and a creditor's legal recourse becomes academic when the creditor *won't* assert his remedy.

Some offshore trusts have been successfully challenged by creditors. In at least one case, the grantor was jailed for contempt. Do you still consider the trust an effective wealth protector?

An offshore trust is only effective if it is structured and administered properly. Still, very few trusts do fail. Those few cases highlight one or more common mistakes:

1) The grantor retained too much control and the court found the trust a sham. For asset protection, you must accept trustee control of your trust, not only in form, but in practice.

2) The trust assets were not outside the United States and could then be seized by a U.S. court who found the transfer to the trust fraudulent.

3) The trust didn't include the necessary protective safeguards or was technically defective.

These mistakes are less likely to occur if the trust is overseen by attorneys experienced with offshore trusts and the recent cases on offshore trusts.

Can a bankruptcy trustee claim offshore trust assets?

A bankruptcy trustee has recovery powers comparable to an individual creditor, and without special treaties has no greater right to claim a bankrupt's former assets transferred to the trust.

However, if the bankruptcy court determines that the offshore transfers were fraudulent, it can deny a bankruptcy discharge, either completely or to the value of the assets transferred. You must truthfully report to the bankruptcy court all recent offshore transfers and any interests in any offshore entity. Of course, a bankruptcy trustee can pursue offshore fraudulent transfers subject to the same obstacles other creditors face. Usually a trustee advantageously settles, rather than pursues offshore litigation.

When bankruptcy is a possibility, it is important to select the right trust haven. British Commonwealth havens, for example, are compelled under Section 426 of the United Kingdom Insolvency Act of 1986 to grant reciprocal enforcement of U.K. and Commonwealth bankruptcy decrees. A United States bankruptcy decree thus entered in the United Kingdom may be enforceable in a Commonwealth haven, such as Belize, Bermuda, British Virgin Islands, Cayman Islands, Gibraltar, and Turks and Caicos. These havens also may not protect against other foreign bankruptcies. A trustee of a trust can relocate offshore trusts to a haven without reciprocal bankruptcy treaties in the eventuality of a settlor's or beneficiary's bankruptcy.

Do offshore trusts protect against the IRS and other agencies?

Even when domestic asset protection adequately protects against other creditors and litigants, it won't necessarily protect against the IRS, who has more powerful remedies. A taxpayer's assets are safest from IRS seizure when sheltered offshore.

Offshore asset protection havens do not enforce IRS levies or summons, or cooperate with IRS efforts to discover or seize assets, without special treaties with the U.S. Nevis and the other havens we recommend do not have such treaties.

You must be very careful when protecting assets from the U.S. government. Candidly discuss your situation with your attorney so you do not violate federal laws impeding the collection of taxes. Offshore asset transfers and legal or beneficial interests in offshore entities must be disclosed to the IRS when they try to enforce collection.

How effective are offshore trusts against governmental seizures and forfeitures?

Offshore protection is the only way to avoid asset forfeiture. Any asset allegedly used in a crime in the U.S. can be seized by the government regardless of ownership. Encumbering assets is the only domestic strategy that can protect against seizure.

Transferring assets offshore derived from a criminal activity constitutes money laundering. And if you are convicted of a crime involving the asset, the unavailability of the asset to help satisfy governmental claims may encourage a judge to sentence you more harshly. While you may protect the asset offshore, this does not necessarily protect its owner.

With so many marriages dissolving, is offshore protection useful in divorce planning?

Unhappy spouses contemplating divorce oftentimes shelter marital assets offshore. However, divorcing spouses must eventually and truthfully disclose their assets to the divorce court. While the divorce court cannot recover and divide offshore assets, the divorce court can award the victimized spouse more U.S.-based assets to compensate for offshore assets held by the other spouse. The court also can grant the injured spouse additional compensatory alimony or support. Offshore protection is best used to shelter assets from a potentially dishonest spouse, not to cheat a spouse.

Can offshore arrangements protect inheritances?

Offshore protective structures can superbly shield anticipated inheritances from creditors of the beneficiary because the inheritance can directly pass to the offshore structure upon the testator's death. Of course, the testator must specifically name the offshore entity as the beneficiary under the will or living trust. We commonly have a client's foreign trust named the beneficiary of the parents' living trust. The testator can also use an *inter vivos* offshore trust, which is funded during the testator's lifetime.

Can an offshore trust protect an estate from a disgruntled heir?

A disgruntled heir cannot easily challenge an offshore trust or impede trust distributions. First, trust affairs are secretive. Second, the disgruntled heir must sue in a foreign haven inhospitable to such claims. Third, the trust, unlike most living trusts, is discretionary. A disgruntled heir cannot force distributions in his own favor, regardless of the outcome of any legal challenge, because the acceptance of a beneficiary and the timing and conditions for distribution are entirely within the trustee's discretion.

An offshore trust is frequently used to avoid the forced heirship laws that compel bequeathing a minimum share of an estate to a spouse or children.

You must establish your trust in a haven that specifically ignores U.S. forced heirship laws, and also have your entire estate in the trust if you are to avoid claims from disgruntled heirs.

Can you improve protection using multiple offshore structures?

If you have considerable money invested offshore, separate structures with different trustees in different havens will provide diversity and add protection. It is more difficult for creditors to seize assets in multiple entities, but also more expensive to establish and maintain. There are tradeoffs. I recommend diversification and different entities when you have over $2 million offshore; however, you must decide for yourself how many eggs you want in any one basket.

How are trust funds invested?

The trustee normally invests as the grantor wishes—provided the investments are prudent for trusts and remain outside the U.S. where your wealth remains safe from creditors.

Whether you prefer annuities, a bank account, gold bullion, a blue-chip mutual fund, or other international investments for your trust, you have the opportunity to invest anywhere and in a wide variety of investments. International investing can be profitable and exciting.

Can an offshore protective structure invest in the U.S.?

U.S. investments are sometimes owned by offshore structures until threatened by creditors, when the domestic investments are exchanged for foreign investments. Start with foreign investments. It's safer. Some trustees will not invest in less protected U.S. assets, because you don't always have advance notice of threats to your assets. Avoid unpleasant surprises. You have less worry with your assets invested offshore.

Avoid investing in Canada, England, and other countries with strong U.S. treaty arrangements. Your investment advisor can advise you on the safest investments.

What are my offshore investment options?

You have about the same offshore investment options as in the U.S., but there is a wider variety of investments offshore. You can invest in stocks, bonds, mutual funds, annuities, money market accounts, precious metals, or simply keep your money in a bank account. By investing offshore, you not only gain creditor protection but also the safety of international diversification. Investing with different currencies can also improve yields.

Avoid investment scams. Offshore bank debenture programs and other deals that sound too good to be true aren't true. The naive and greedy usually lose their investment. Retain a reputable investment advisor and buy only "blue chip" offshore investments. Our firm can recommend several highly reputable offshore investment advisors.

Can I control my trust investments?

The trustee can appoint you an investment advisor to the trust and, in that capacity, you can operate a separate discretionary account under your sole control and directly make investments on behalf of the trust. You can use U.S. brokers, but for maximum protection it is safest to trade through foreign brokers. You would not remain as the investment advisor when under creditor attack.

How do you find a good foreign investment advisor?

You will find excellent investment advisors in every haven. The foreign investment advisors and asset management firms I recommend have performed well and obtained excellent results for my clients. Scrutinize prospective advisors carefully. Don't rely upon their marketing information. Check backgrounds and affiliations, obtain references, and start with a minimal investment until you test their performance. We can also recommend offshore brokerage and trading firms for both U.S. and international investments. Most investment advisory contracts can be terminated on short notice, so there is always an opportunity to change advisors when their advisory performance is unsatisfactory.

Can an offshore trust own a U.S. business or real estate?

An American corporation or LLC should own and operate a U.S.-based business. The trust can own the shares or membership interest in this U.S. entity. Similarly, real estate should be titled to a U.S. limited partnership or LLC owned by the trust.

Can an offshore trust own life insurance?

The offshore trust is the ideal way to own life insurance. Upon your death, the proceeds will be estate tax free. It also establishes creditor protection for the insurance proceeds, free of claims from creditors of the grantor or beneficiaries. If both spouses are insured (a second to die policy), the insurance proceeds in the offshore trust can benefit their children or grandchildren and possibly avoid U.S. taxes.

Can the offshore trust own a pension or IRA?

Retirement plans must remain titled in the pension or IRA custodial account; however, the offshore trust can be the beneficiary and thus protect distributions.

Will transfers of assets to the trust be taxable?

No. A properly drafted grantor trust is tax neutral. There are no capital gains or gift taxes on transfers to the trust.

How can funds be safely repatriated when you have creditors?

Repatriated funds are, of course, vulnerable to U.S. creditors. During the duress, you wouldn't repatriate more funds than you need.

There are several safe ways to access offshore funds: 1) Foreign trustees can directly pay your bills. 2) Funds may be repatriated to a protective domestic spendthrift trust and then disbursed to you. 3) You can transfer repatriated funds to a third party account for temporary protection. 4) A spouse or other close relative can be a trust co-beneficiary and receive and expend funds from the trust on your behalf. 5) Finally, you can access offshore funds through an offshore "debit" card and through U.S.-based ATM machines— about $1,000 daily. With the debit card, you can also charge purchases as with any Visa or Master Card.

Can my trust issue to me an offshore credit card?

Offshore credit cards are usually debit cards or secured credit cards. An offshore debit card is a convenient way to access offshore funds, but the trustee must control the available credit and retain the right to terminate the card. Otherwise, a court may conclude you have unlimited access to the trust assets, and you lose asset protection.

Are distributions from the offshore trust taxable?

No. Trust earnings are taxed to the grantor in the year earned. Therefore, distributions are without further taxes. A beneficiary who receives a distribution after the grantor dies pays a tax on accumulated earnings from the date of the grantor's death. There are no taxes due the trust haven because they are "no tax" jurisdictions.

What are the reporting requirements for an offshore trust?

U.S. law requires the grantor or beneficiary of any foreign trust to disclose the trust's creation, transfers of assets to the trust, and notice of death of the grantor. Any U.S. beneficiary who obtains a distribution from the trust must file a tax return disclosing the trust name and distribution received.

The trustee must also appoint a U.S.-based agent to receive financial information concerning the trust and to receive and reply to IRS notices. The grantor must file with the IRS the name of the U.S. agent. The trust must have a taxpayer I.D. number and complete and annually submit IRS Form # 3520-A. Trust reporting requirements are not complicated. Always comply with trust and other offshore reporting requirements to avoid severe IRS penalties. Canada and England have similar trust reporting requirements. Reports are confidential and cannot be subpoenaed in a lawsuit.

Can you save estate taxes with an offshore trust?

Assets in an offshore trust with a U.S. beneficiary are included in the estate of the U.S. grantor, subject to the allowed estate tax exclusion. However, if the offshore trust receives the assets under the grantor's last will, the income earned by the trust assets accumulate tax-deferred until distributed to the U.S. beneficiaries. Tax deferred distributions can build faster wealth.

Through careful planning, you can remove the trust from your estate to reduce estate taxes. You can use the trust as a credit shelter trust, for Crummey gifts, or as a Q-tip trust. There are many more ways to use the trust to reduce estate taxes but, because the strategies are complex, they are best discussed with your tax advisor.

Can the offshore trust replace a living trust?

Possibly. You would use the living trust to bequeath U.S.-based assets and the offshore trust to bequeath offshore assets. These trusts frequently have different assets and perhaps also different beneficiaries. You can use these trusts in combination. For example, upon your death, your living trust assets may be transferred to the offshore trust. If all your assets were in your offshore trust, there would be no need for a domestic living trust or will. Do not complete an estate plan without considering the potential role of an offshore trust as a part of your plan.

Can you revoke or terminate an offshore trust?

The offshore trust is irrevocable and cannot be revoked or terminated. However, your trust may allow the protector and trustee together to revoke the trust. You can, however, borrow or distribute the entire trust assets to beneficiaries to empty the trust. Or, you can disqualify the trust by not paying the annual filing fees. A trust doesn't commit you to future expenses.

Can I use my offshore trust to encumber U.S. assets?

Absolutely, and this strategy is oftentimes part of a comprehensive asset protection plan. There are many ways to structure the transaction, but the net effect is to create a valid mortgage against your U.S. assets. This equity stripping leaves nothing for a U.S. creditor to seize and may, in certain circumstances, allow you to deduct interest on your taxes. The offshore mortgage program is a powerful wealth preservation strategy when used properly.

What happens to the trust assets when the grantor dies?

The trust assets are distributed according to the trust provisions and the grantor's requests in the statement of wishes.

The offshore trust is usually *inter vivos* and operates during the grantor's lifetime. It can instead be a *testamentary* trust and activate or continue beyond your lifetime to efficiently and safely transfer your wealth to your designated beneficiaries. The offshore trust is quite versatile for estate planning.

The trust ordinarily dissolves upon the grantor's death or after a fixed period thereafter, but the term can be extended if the grantor's estate or a beneficiary has creditor problems and needs continued trust protection.

Can an offshore trust save income taxes?

The most common offshore trust for Americans is the *grantor* trust. The grantor trust is tax neutral. The trust itself pays no tax as all trust income is taxed directly to the grantor in the year earned. There is no tax deferral. The grantor trust then is taxed like an S Corporation, a limited partnership, or a living trust. The offshore trust offers neither tax advantages nor disadvantages for an American grantor.

MORE OFFSHORE WEALTH PROTECTION STRATEGIES

4

What are some alternatives to the offshore trust?

I frequently recommend the Nevis LLC for my offshore clients. However, in certain cases, I still use the offshore trust, particularly if the client needs offshore estate planning, or if there would be tax consequences from transferring appreciated assets to an offshore entity other than an offshore trust. Of course, other entities can be considered, and more are being developed, promoted and used for asset protection. Undoubtedly, we will have still better future options. Other present options include the Bahamian limited partnership, private foundations, hybrid companies, or LLCs from other countries.

Explain the Nevis LLC.

Nevis, a small Caribbean and British Commonwealth nation in the Leeward Islands, has in recent years gained a national reputation for financial privacy and asset protection. The Nevis LLC is its newest wealth preservation weapon.

Most states and many foreign jurisdictions recognize limited liability companies; however, the Nevis LLC is particularly effective for asset protection due to its many unique and advantageous features. It combines the protective advantages of the offshore trust, American limited partnership, and Nevada corporation. It is a remarkable entity. We have a special report on the Nevis LLC for interested readers.

How do you structure the Nevis LLC?

The Nevis LLC can be either member directed or managed by a foreign director. For asset protection, the LLC would be controlled by a foreign (Nevis) managing director. Contributors to the LLC become the LLC members, who are similar to stockholders in a corporation or limited partners in a limited partnership. They own the LLC but do not directly manage it. Managerial control rests with the managing director. Through this transfer of control you protect the contributed assets from U.S. court orders.

How does the Nevis LLC protect against creditors?

Conceptually, the Nevis LLC functions much like an offshore trust and U.S. limited partnership. The LLC member no longer owns his contributed assets, which is now owned by the LLC. The LLC member cannot be ordered by a court to repatriate these contributed assets, because all powers concerning the LLC now rest with a managing director beyond U.S. court control. The creditor of a debtor-member can only obtain a charging order against the member's LLC interest, which entitles the creditor only to the debtor-member's share of any profit or liquidation distributions from the LLC. The member's LLC interest cannot be seized by the creditor, nor can the creditor vote or exercise other member rights, such as inspect books and records.

Any U.S. court order to transfer or seize the debtor-member's LLC interest would be ignored by the managing director who, under Nevis law, would only recognize a creditor's charging order obtainable in the Nevis courts.

Obviously, if a debtor-member has a major interest in the LLC, the managing director would not distribute profits seizable by his charging order creditor. If the debtor-member has a small interest, and withholding distributions would conflict with the interests of the other debtor-members, the minority debtor-member may title his LLC interest with another self-owned Nevis LLC as a safe reservoir for the debtor-member's distributed profits. In practice, a debtor-member can usually access LLC funds without classifying it a "distribution of profits." Payments as salaries (e.g., as investment advisor), loans, etc. are not subject to the charging order.

Both Nevis law and the IRS Code impose U.S. income tax liability on the charging order creditor for the debtor-member's share of profits, attributable to the debtor-member. The charging order creditor incurs tax liability even if the creditor received no distribution. These "poison pill" protective features also are found with U.S. limited partnerships and LLCs, but not with other offshore entities.

A properly-structured Nevis LLC delegates all important powers to the managing director who, like a trustee of an offshore trust, will ignore U.S. court orders to repatriate assets. If the LLC has two or more members, a well-drafted operating agreement will require unanimous member vote to change the managing director. This overcomes any court order compelling one debtor-member to replace the director to one appointed by the court for purposes of repatriating LLC assets. The Nevis LLC thus has about same protective "duress" characteristics of the offshore trust, except that the debtor-member retains an interest in the LLC and, derivatively, its assets.

Which is more protective, the Nevis LLC or an offshore trust?

I consider a properly-structured Nevis LLC more protective, particularly if you have existing creditors, where a transfer to the trust would be a fraudulent conveyance and contestable in the trust haven.

If a Nevis LLC member has an existing creditor, the Nevis LLC ordinance allows the member to transfer his assets to the LLC without it constituting a fraudulent conveyance. If the member's interest is proportionate to his share of the contributed capital, it is then a fair value exchange for adequate consideration and exempt from the Nevis fraudulent transfers statutes. Interestingly, a promise of a future contribution by existing or incoming LLC members can be used to measure proportionality. The debtor-member can then own minority interest subject to the charging order, although he contributed all or most of the LLC's present assets. This dilution strategy effectively discourages charging order requests and is a feature unique to the Nevis LLC. U.S. limited partnership law is unsettled on whether a present creditor can successfully recover a transfer to a limited partnership as a fraudulent conveyance, even if the debtor received, in exchange for his contributed assets, a proportionate interest in the limited partnership. (Some courts say that creditor impairment is sufficient for a fraudulent transfer.) There is no ambiguity under Nevis law. Investing in a properly-structured Nevis LLC is thus not a fraudulent transfer, and not challengeable by an *existing* creditor.

In this one important respect, I consider the Nevis LLC more protective than a foreign trust, domestic limited partnership or domestic LLC. And it is more legally and ethically defensible regardless of the financial situation of a contributing member. This point cannot be overlooked at a time when offshore trusts receiving fraudulently transferred assets are increasingly susceptible to successful attack or stern court sanctions against their grantors.

The Nevis LLC is certainly a more attractive option for attorneys whose clients have existing creditors and concerns about professional responsibility and liability arising from a fraudulent transfer to a trust or another protective structure.

Of course, lawyers disagree on most issues, and the offshore trust has its supporters who claim its protection is superior. That is why, in my more serious cases, I maximize protection and use a Nevis LLC as the grantor of an offshore trust. My client then has the best of both worlds.

Are there other advantages with the Nevis LLC?

The Nevis LLC boasts several other significant benefits:

- The Nevis LLC has minimal reporting requirements and is not subject to U.S. foreign trust reporting requirements. A U.S. member with a 10% or greater LLC interest still has foreign corporation ownership reporting requirements to the IRS.

- Although tax neutral, the Nevis LLC can elect to be taxed either as a partnership or "C" Corporation. Nevis imposes no taxes on the LLC.

- The LLC can be structured for profits to flow to the members in any proportion specified in the operating agreement. This proportion may differ from their ownership interest.

- Ownership can be in registered or bearer form for anonymity.

- A protector can be appointed over the managing director, as with OAPTs.

- The LLC agreement can include anti-creditor "poison pills." For example, members may have their interests assessable by the managing director against a charging order creditor.

- The LLC operating agreement may include a "flight" or "Cuba clause," allowing the manager to expatriate threatened LLC assets to a successor protective structure in another asset protection haven.

- Managing directors of the Nevis LLC are immune from company liability, and creditors cannot pierce the corporate veil.

- Nevis does not require minute books, annual director or member meetings, or other customary corporate formalities.

- As with domestic FLP and LLCs, the Nevis LLC can similarly save estate and gift taxes through discounted valuations. Members can also gift ownership interests in their Nevis LLC and still retain full income rights and management or voting control.

- The Nevis LLC can be owned by an offshore trust in place of an IBC, or in combination with domestic entities such as FLPs and irrevocable trusts to coordinate domestic and offshore estate and asset protection planning.

- Nevis LLCs can be set up quickly and are usually less costly to organize and maintain than offshore asset protection trusts.

- Nevis is politically and economically stable, uses the U.S. dollar as its currency, and has excellent banking, financial, and fiduciary services.

- American LLCs with fewer protective features, are easily converted to Nevis LLCs. This may not be advantageous for an LLC with U.S. assets.

The Nevis LLC may in many cases replace the offshore asset protection trust, but in certain instances the offshore trust is still best for offshore wealth protection, estate planning, forced heirship avoidance, or other special purposes achievable only through a trust. Transfers of appreciated U.S. assets to the Nevis LLC are subject to a 35% excise tax on the appreciated amount. This tax is avoided with transfers to a U.S. grantor trust.

The Nevis LLC is a worthy upgrade from foreign IBCs which offer considerably less protection and no reciprocal advantages.

The Nevis LLC is a pioneer of newer entities, and more havens will seek legislation for establishing protective structures other than the OAPT. The Bahamas, for example, has new limited partnership laws closely modeled after the Nevis LLC. Bahamas, Liechtenstein, and Panama have private foundations. St. Vincent and Isle of Man hybrid companies can be substitutes for a trust and alternatives to the Nevis LLC. The search for "the better mousetrap" will continue, however, only an exceptionally innovative jurisdiction can create a "mousetrap" superior to the Nevis LLC.

Let's move on to some other possibilities. Alaska and Delaware have enacted "asset protection" trust laws. How protective are Alaska or Delaware trusts?

I do not recommend Alaska or Delaware trusts for asset protection, although they have some estate planning advantages.

Alaska and Delaware must recognize judgments and court orders from other states. If a California court, for instance, ruled that assets were fraudulently transferred to an Alaskan trust, Alaska is constitutionally bound to recognize both the California judgment and re-transfer orders.

While the same creditor may attack a fraudulent transfer to an offshore trust, the creditor must first again litigate the case in the trust haven (which never recognizes foreign judgments) and, subsequently, file a separate fraudulent conveyance action in the trust haven. These procedural roadblocks don't exist with Alaska and Delaware, which, in my view, promote a comparatively poor protective structure to attract capital from Americans in other states too frightened to entrust their wealth offshore.

U.S. limited partnerships are popular for protecting domestic assets. Are international limited partnerships more protective?

A limited partnership in the Isle of Man or Bahamas is preferable to domestic limited partnerships if the assets are offshore and beyond reach of U.S. courts. They have no advantage for U.S.-based assets still within the jurisdiction of U.S. courts. Moreover, you incur a 35% excise tax liability if you transfer appreciated assets to these entities. The Nevis LLC is quite similar to these foreign limited partnerships but offers several advantages. Like the Nevis LLC, foreign LPs will also gain in popularity over the offshore trust.

Many foreign IBCs' organizers recommend them for asset protection. Do you agree?

No. An IBC (foreign corporation) can privatize your offshore wealth, but privacy is not asset protection. A creditor who discovers you invested in an offshore company can have the court order you to transfer your IBC ownership to the creditor or liquidate its assets for the benefit of the creditor. Courts won't believe you "gifted" the money or that it somehow "disappeared." Asset protection needs a structure designed for that purpose, not an IBC. Promoters of IBCs should not consider asset protection one of its benefits.

Can I secretly own "bearer" shares in an offshore company?

Bearer shares may sound like a good idea; however, you are considered the owner if the shares are in your possession, and you commit perjury if you conceal this. For asset protection, use an offshore trust or another structure specifically designed for protection.

How do foreign foundations compare to offshore trusts?

Civil law jurisdictions recognize foundations. Trusts are recognized in common-law countries. Liechtenstein and Panama both use family foundations and the Bahamas will shortly. The foundation works similar to the trust. The foundation has no shareholders, partners, owners, or members— only beneficiaries and a director or managing council that manages the foundation as a trustee administers a trust, or a managing director the LLC.

Foundations provide good secrecy and asset protection comparable to the trust. The foundation can be created by express deed or a will. Unlike a U.S. charitable foundation, it need not have a charitable purpose. Liechtenstein and Panama foundations are particularly interesting and, when structured properly, can possibly also reduce income and estate taxes.

One major drawback with the foundation is that Americans are still unfamiliar with these entities, and there is comparatively little law to guide us on their safety. Foundations can become more advantageous if trusts become more vulnerable to creditors and the U.S. Government imposes more burdensome reporting requirements on them.

Can owning a private international bank help to protect assets?

Bank ownership won't materially enhance asset protection. You can, however, gain some tax benefits and financing opportunities through private bank ownership. A private bank will cost about $50,000 to establish and $15,000 annually to maintain, plus considerable time and effort to operate and promote. Unless you are experienced in banking and have $500,000 or more to invest, private bank ownership probably won't pay.

How do "Pure" trusts or "common law" trusts compare to offshore trusts?

For a trust to protect assets, it must be irrevocable, and the settlor cannot retain significant control.

Obviously, an "offshore" trust must also must be established under the trust laws of a foreign jurisdiction. Pure trusts promoters make unsupported claims that their trusts can avoid taxes and creditor claims, which is generally untrue. The IRS considers pure trusts "abusive" trusts, and they can cause serious tax consequences. Nor are pure trusts necessarily creditor-protected. Even when they provide some protection, you can usually obtain greater protection with other structures. Avoid so-called "pure trusts."

What about a Nevada Corporation for asset protection?

Nevada has excellent corporate laws, but a Nevada Corporation (or a corporation in any other state) isn't your answer for rock-solid creditor protection. Nevada corporate promoters tout privacy when the Nevada Corporation issues bearer shares, but privacy is never protection. The Nevada Corporation can play a supporting role in an asset protection plan, but a good plan never relies upon it as the foundation for protection.

What plan or structure do you generally recommend?

Asset protection planning must be customized to fit your specific needs and circumstances. Some plans are simple, others complex. You must consider the full range of structures, havens, and strategies to design the plan best for you.

We do commonly combine the U.S. limited partnership with an offshore trust as its limited partner. This balances the desire to retain control with trust protection. Another popular arrangement is an offshore trust investing in Swiss variable annuities. This maximizes protection, privacy, and tax deferral with a solid investment. A Nevis LLC can well serve the offshore objectives for most offshore investors. Whether these or other arrangements are best for you must be decided with your professional advisors.

Are Swiss annuities protected from lawsuits?

Yes. Under Swiss insurance law, Swiss insurance policies and annuities cannot be seized by creditors. The Swiss annuity enjoys built-in protection against all creditors and judgments, including every type litigation, creditor claim, IRS claim, governmental forfeiture orders, bankruptcy, and divorce decrees. No other investment, and few asset protection arrangements, give more absolute protection.

How are Swiss annuities protected?

Article 81 of the Swiss Insurance Act provides the Swiss annuity cannot be seized by a policyholder's creditor. Upon creditor attack, the beneficiaries become the substitute policyholder and acquires all rights to the policy. No court can then compel the policyholder to liquidate the annuity or repatriate the annuity proceeds, as it is no longer within his power to do so. Since title to the annuity automatically passes to the beneficiary upon a policyholder's bankruptcy, the trustee acquires no title or claim. The policyholder or a beneficiary must notify the insurance company of any foreseeable danger, such as a lawsuit or bankruptcy, so the insurance company is prepared to protect the policy.

Certain requirements must be followed for Swiss annuity protection:The annuity policyholder must designate his or her spouse or descendants (children, grandchildren, etc.) as the beneficiary. A third party must be a irrevocable beneficiary. The beneficiary designation must be made at least one year before bankruptcy or attempted creditor seizure of the policy. A Swiss annuity is therefore unprotected within the first year of ownership. It is obviously important to purchase the Swiss annuity well in advance of a creditor claim.

How to Protect Your Money Offshore

Are beneficiaries of a Swiss annuity protected?

Beneficiaries under a Swiss annuity have their annuity payments protected from their creditors if the beneficiary receives funds from the annuity without having compensated the policyholder, the insurance company, or any third party for such payments.

Are Swiss annuities automatically safe from creditors after one year?

A Swiss annuity is not necessarily creditor-proof after one year. If a policyholder buys a Swiss annuity with the intent to protect against present creditors, it can be voided by these creditors if at the time of transfer: 1) the beneficiaries knew of this actual intent, 2) the policyholder later files bankruptcy or has his assets subject to seizure, and his other assets do not cover his liabilities, and 3) a creditor files the fraudulent transfer claim within five (5) years of purchasing the annuity purchase.

There are, however, several major obstacles to recovery. One is a creditor's difficulty proving actual knowledge by the beneficiaries concerning the policyholder's intent. A child has less imputed

136

knowledge of a parent's financial objectives than a spouse, and is thus a safer beneficiary under these circumstances. The creditor must also prove the policyholder could reasonably anticipate insolvency when the annuity was purchased.

The policyholder's creditor also faces serious procedural blocks. Proceedings to seize an annuity must be in Switzerland. While the Swiss enforce foreign judgments, the creditor must still undergo a long multi-step route to seize the annuity. A bankruptcy trustee has less procedural difficulty. Switzerland routinely enforces foreign bankruptcy decrees that coincide with Swiss law, but Swiss annuities cannot be lost in a foreign bankruptcy unless a voidable preference under Swiss fraudulent conveyance rules.

The Swiss Debt Collection and Bankruptcy Act considers a gift a voidable preference if made within one year from the date of the creditor asserted a claim against the annuity, or the policyholder filed bankruptcy

Who should own the Swiss annuity?

Swiss insurance companies generally won't sell a Swiss annuity directly to an American, but will issue a policy to a foreign IBC, LLC, or trust established by an American.

My clients typically buy their annuity through an asset protection structure—usually an offshore asset protection trust. The trust protection adds to the annuity protection provided by Swiss law. The trust becomes the annuity owner and the irrevocable beneficiary. Through trust ownership, the annuity is immediately protected and, after one year, gains added protection under Swiss law.

Although the trust would be the irrevocable beneficiary, you can name the beneficiaries of the trust and thus retain the flexibility to re-designate beneficiaries without losing protection. A Swiss annuity owned by an offshore trust creates an exceptionally strong wealth protection plan.

Can a U.S. judge order the owner of a Swiss annuity to liquidate the annuity?

If the policyholder attempts to redeem the policy under duress (court order), the order will be ignored by the Swiss insurance company. Of course, the policyholder or beneficiary should advise the insurance company of any anticipated attack against the annuity. Since the annuity will usually be owned by the offshore trust, the trustee must order the liquidation and repatriation—an unlikely event if your creditors would seize the proceeds.

Can IRA accounts be rolled into Swiss annuities?

They can only if the Swiss annuity qualifies for rollover and the U.S. custodian accepts the annuity as an investment. IRAs and other self-directed retirement accounts are excellent candidates for Swiss annuities. Most states don't fully creditor-protect these retirement accounts, and even ERISA qualified plans are vulnerable to IRS claims because they cannot be owned by asset protection structures. Rollover into a Swiss annuity essentially allows the retirement account to import Swiss protection.

How do Swiss annuities compare to U.S. annuities?

As with American annuities, Swiss annuities are either fixed or variable. Fixed annuities guarantee you a fixed return, usually over your lifetime. Variable annuities are essentially investments in mutual funds or stocks wrapped in an insurance contract. Its value fluctuates.

Swiss annuities have many advantages over U.S. annuities:

- Swiss annuities are creditor-protected. U.S. annuities are only protected in a few states and unprotected in divorce or against the IRS.

- Swiss annuities are not subject to U.S. court orders.

- Swiss insurance companies are more financially secure than American insurers.

- Swiss annuities are private.

- Swiss annuities can be denominated in Swiss francs and other currencies besides the U.S. dollar.

- Swiss annuities are not considered a foreign account subject to U.S. reporting.

- Swiss annuities are exempt from the 35% withholding tax on foreign-held Swiss bank accounts.

- Swiss annuities are U.S. taxed deferred.

The Swiss variable annuity is both an excellent investment and formidable wealth protector for nationals of any country. Consider it for your investment portfolio. Unfortunately, because most Americans are unaware of their benefits, the Swiss annuity is seldom utilized by Americans for investment and asset protection. Nevertheless, it can be *your* key to both sounder wealth-building and wealth preservation. We have a complete report on Swiss annuities and the names of several Swiss insurance companies.

Why do so few Americans own Swiss annuities?

Swiss annuities cannot be sold within the U.S., so U.S. financial planners or investment brokers cannot sell them. You must go offshore to buy them.As an American wealth protection attorney, I believe too few professional advisors— including my colleagues in asset protection law—consider Swiss annuities for asset protection. Lawyers may be too preoccupied with forming more profitable legal structures to suggest a Swiss annuity, which may offer equal or even better protection but pays nothing to the lawyer. Combining Swiss annuities with an asset protection trust can produce the one best wealth preservation plans for most Americans.

Can you set up your own private offshore annuity for asset protection?

Absolutely. If you have creditors, you can protect your assets by exchanging it for a private annuity. You would first establish a foreign trust for protection and transfer your cash or other property to the trust in exchange for the trust's (or a subsidiary IBC's) unsecured promise to make annual payments to you for the balance of your lifetime. Properly structured foreign private annuities may also help you defer capital gains taxes upon the sale of appreciated assets.

When you exchange an asset for a promise of future payment (the annuity), you receive "fair value" and thus, the transaction is not a fraudulent transfer. The creditor may claim annuity payments, but the prospects of waiting years for payment is unattractive to most creditors.

Do other countries besides Switzerland creditor-protect their annuities?

The Isle of Man and Bahamas provide some statutory protection for their annuities. Nevertheless, I recommend Swiss annuities for creditor protection, because Swiss insurance law offers the broadest protection, and Swiss insurers are the most financially stable.

GETTING STARTED

Dr. Goldstein, how can I decide whether going offshore is right for me?

For all its benefits, offshore wealth protection is not for everyone. You must be realistic about what offshore protection can do for you, and what it can accomplish may not justify its cost or effort.

Candidly discuss your situation with the right professional. Nothing can replace a personal, professional evaluation.

You are not a good offshore candidate if you cannot become comfortable with assets controlled by others. Many people who would benefit greatly from offshore protection don't, for this reason.

Most people eventually overcome their fears or have no choice but to go offshore if they want well-protected wealth. Cautiously they take the plunge. Others never overcome their uneasiness. Nothing can coax them offshore. You also may be uncomfortable with your wealth offshore. Decide whether it is only a matter of learning more or chronic insecurity. If you may refuse offshore protection for less protective domestic asset protection, it may be a mistake. Never compromise asset protection.

How do you implement an offshore wealth protection program?

My professional role involves frequent client conferences, extensive correspondence with the foreign advisors, preparation of numerous documents, investigation of unique problems or issues, and overseeing the transfer of assets, while generally making certain that everything is coordinated and proceeding smoothly. Most importantly, we design a plan to also protect U.S.-based assets and coordinated with his estate plan.

I start with a thorough review of my client's affairs, including present or possible claims. From this information, I can select the appropriate haven and structures and recruit prospective trustees and other foreign professionals to administer the program.

We next design the offshore structure, often combining one or two trusts, IBCs, limited liability companies, or limited partnerships. Proper organizational structure involves many factors. We then draft the numerous documents customized to the special needs of the client. Finally, we assist the client in transferring assets offshore and, when requested, prepare reporting tax forms.

After the plan is implemented, we annually review the client's program and whether it still adequately meets his goals and needs.

How can I learn more about offshore wealth protection?

Educate yourself! Read! There are many good books and journals on offshore investing.

Garrett Publishing has a number of excellent books on asset protection, privacy, and offshore finance. Request their most recent catalog by writing: Garrett Publishing, 384 South Military Trail, Deerfield Beach, Florida, 33442, or phone (954) 480-8543, or visit their website: www.garrettpub.com

If there is one book to read, what else could it possibly be but my very own book *Offshore Havens*? This best seller reveals how the offshore world really works. You will find it at most bookstores, or order directly from Garrett Publishing (see the back of this book). Also check out my forthcoming book *Offshore Wealth: Secrets and Strategies for Global Protection, Privacy, and Wealthbuilding*.

Talk to people! More Americans have offshore wealth protection programs than you might expect. Your professional advisors can probably put you in touch with a few, or call me for the names of clients who will candidly talk to you about their offshore experience.

Most people have common questions, experiences, and fears. How safe will my money be? Will the trustee run away with my money or lose it on some crazy investment? Can I *really* get my money back if I need it? These undoubtedly typify your concerns. That's why you must talk to people who had your same concerns. You will not only find them quite satisfied with their offshore experience, but also find their wealth safe and secure. I consistently hear such comments as this from one client: "You never realize how vulnerable your wealth is here in the U.S.—until it is safely sheltered offshore." Or a comment from a Los Angeles physician: "Before, I was nervous about my money offshore; now I get nervous thinking how easily I could have lost it here."

Knowledge builds confidence and confidence prompts action. That's why I try to educate my clients. It builds confidence. Your offshore program gets under way with more enthusiasm and functions more smoothly when their fears are calmed. When you are informed, you no longer see the venture as a journey on uncharted waters. You know what to expect. Your questions are answered. Your concerns are resolved. And that is why I assisted with this book. I want to help people like yourself build a more secure financial future.

How do you find the right offshore professional advisors?

There is no substitute for good professional advice. By educating yourself, you can more *intelligently* select your advisors and work with them more effectively.

Most offshore professionals are honest, trustworthy and knowledgeable, but every business has its incompetents. My profession is no exception. Start with an attorney experienced in offshore wealth protection. Avoid boilerplate plans or structures from non-lawyers or offshore companies who are not well recommended or sell worthless documents and false information to an unsuspecting public. Your attorney must also coordinate your offshore program with your domestic asset protection and estate planning program.

A lawyer's license doesn't ensure competence but, at least, implies sufficient honesty to stay licensed. Still, an inexperienced lawyer is inadequate and possibly dangerous. Offshore planning involves complex legal, financial, and tax issues. Your attorney will know little about these technical matters unless he or she is well experienced *and* abreast of the rapidly changing offshore rules and strategies.

Check your attorney's references, but respect confidentiality. Never pry into another client's financial affairs. Is your prospective lawyer a member of the Offshore Institute? Active offshore specialists usually belong to this worldwide organization, whose members have high professional standards and offshore experience.

Bar associations do not maintain rosters of offshore lawyers; however, your regular attorney may find you one by inquiring within legal circles. Can I assist you? I have affiliated offices in several major cities and clients in nearly *every* state. I also work closely with attorneys, accountants, financial planners, and other professionals whose clients require offshore protection. Whether you are a prospective client or a professional whose clients can benefit from our services—we look forward to working with you.

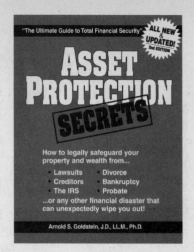

INDEX

A-F

Alaska and Delaware trusts 128
Alternatives to offshore trusts 119
Asset protection entities.. 79
Asset protection plan 33
Assets 25, 42
Bankruptcy... 24, 100
Banks.. 54
Bearer shares 130
Beneficiaries.. 83, 91
Common law trusts 132
Countries with havens 54, 82, 142
"Deep pockets" 26
Disclosure 72
Disgruntled heir.. 104
Divorce 24, 103
Encumber.. 114
FAPT... 75
Features of havens 49, 50, 52
Fees 36
Financial disasters 29
Financial privacy 63
Foreign banks.. 69
Foreign foundations 131
Fraudulent transfer 95, 97
Future creditor.. 40

G-O

Grantor 82, 83, 92

Grantor's death 114

Havens 54, 66

IBC 75, 130

Illegal protection 34, 63

Inheritance 103

Insurance 28

Investment advisor 108

Investments 105, 106, 107

Irrevocable trust 80

IRS 58, 73, 101

Lawsuits 23

Liability insurance 27

Limited partnership 46, 129

Living trust 113

MLAT 67

Multiple offshore structures 105

Nevada Corporation 133

Nevis LLC 75, 119, 125

Offshore asset protection 43

Offshore credit card 110

Offshore haven 41, 47

Offshore secrecy laws 65

Offshore strategies 32

Offshore trust 79

Offshore wealth protection program 146

P-S

Privacy..73
Private offshore annuity 142
Professional advisor 29, 149
Protection...38
Protector 83, 89
Pure trusts 132
Repatriation 96, 110
Reporting requirements 111
Revoking a trust...113
Safety..69
Secrecy...66, 68, 93
Seizure of assets..98, 102
Selecting a protector...90
Selecting a trustee 82, 87
Stability 53
Straw 40
Swiss annuities...134
    and American annuities...............................139
    beneficiaries...136
    creditors 136
    IRA accounts...139
    liquidation 138
    protection...134
    who should own 137

T-W

Taxes 111, 112, 115

Terminate 113

Threats 23

Titling assets..74

Transfer 43, 71

Trusts 79

Trust-owned assets 108

Trustee powers..84

Wealth preservation lawyer 37

Wealth protection..23